BOUTIQUE *Home*

10 STEPS TO CREATING YOUR BOUTIQUE SPACE

SUE McGREGOR

BOOKS

DEDICATED TO:

My parents, for the wonderful homes they created. Their legacy of heart and home has inspired my career.

My nieces, nephews and god-children, and in loving memory of my sister-in-law Jeanie.

Boutique Home
10 Steps To Creating Your Boutique Home © Sue McGregor
ISBN paperback: 978-1-909116-06-1

Published in 2014 by SRA Books

Illustrations © Lucy Daniels, Dippy Egg Illustrations

Photography, pp 56, 78, 90, 116 & 132 by John West, john@asaphotoservices.co.uk

Printed in the UK by Latimer Trend, Plymouth

Contents

 YOUR BOUTIQUE HOME

You know how it feels when you return from holiday, having stayed in the perfect boutique hotel in the perfect location, only to return to your reality of home. Living the dream lasted just a few days or weeks.

As you cast your eye over your home, the familiar excuses of changing it for the better go something like this:

'It's too expensive to change – I'd rather spend that on a holiday.'

'I'm hardly here so why should I care?'

'I really don't have the time or energy to deal with it.'

'There's so much to do and I don't know where to start.'

Remember that where you are living is also a part of your journey, and your home reflects who you are and how you wish to live.

So how does your existing environment make you feel? Does it express the real you?

If you had the ability and know-how to transform your environment into a space you would enjoy and be proud to live in, what would it look like?

I believe we all deserve to express our true selves and live our own dream. I have written this pocket-size book to help you achieve just this. My mission and work in life is to transform people's lives, realising their dream home and lifestyle.

I have written *Boutique Home* as a clear, simple and logical 10-step process, to guide you through developing your home from start to finish.

I've worked for 25 years as an interior designer and during that time I have visited and designed some beautiful spaces, but the ones I feel most happy to return to are those that convey a clear expression of who the client is and their lifestyle. I always loved returning to my parents' home in Queensland, Australia – the house had been built around the concept of a Fijian *bure* and suited the open, relaxed and welcoming atmosphere my parents shared with friends and family.

The entrance opened up to a large living/dining area, which expanded across the width of the space and was separated by a glass wall from a lush, tropical garden with a rock pool. The interior, clad in cedar and slate, continued the natural theme. This combination of materials also created a cool, quiet sanctuary. Another major focal point was the handcrafted, spiral cedar staircase and the furniture designed from tree roots. To my mind, the design is timeless; the perfect resolution to lifestyle, aspect and climate.

Your culture, family, life experiences and aspirations are all significant factors when evaluating what you want in your home. This history is your uniqueness and your value. So feel proud to express who you are, what means most to you and the items you love – from the minimal to baroque!

To enable you to work on the exercises for your project, I have included a case study that you can follow and refer to throughout the book. The Jeffries' case study is a largish project, but please remember that, whether it is a one-bedroom flat or five-bedroom house, the principles for a project are relevant to both.

The Jeffries family want to encapsulate that boutique hotel environment. Sally and Peter Jeffries live with their two children, Oliver (18) and Claire (14), in Notting Hill – a fashionable area of London that mixes style, culture and lovely Victorian architecture.

Peter works for a large media organisation and enjoys collecting art and books. Sally works from home, writes a weekly column for a magazine and enjoys restoring furniture as a hobby.

They enjoy family life and a relaxed mode of entertaining friends and clients, both indoors and outdoors.

They have a collection of art, including sculpture, which they want incorporated into the scheme. Their preference is for natural finishes of wood and stone.

This is what the Jeffries' brief looked like:

....

THE JEFFRIES' HOME

Approximately 3000 sq ft (278.709 sq m), 4-bed, Grade II listed Victorian house, consisting of a combined living-dining area, separate kitchen, four bedrooms, three bathrooms and a WC. The staircase, internal doors, architraves and cornice detailing are original. The fireplace in the living room is original. Ceiling height is about 15 ft (4500 mm) on the first floor and ground floors. The second floor is approximately 10 ft high (approx. 3000 mm). The building condition appears to be in good order, with a few slight cracks that will have to be checked.

BRIEF

The Jeffries' request is for the living and kitchen areas to be combined, creating a formal and informal seating area. All bathrooms to be updated and en suites to be created. The master bedroom will also require a dressing room.

The existing finishes, which are true to the period of the building, are to be retained and restored, particularly in the entrance hallway. The existing carpet in the living areas is to be replaced with engineered parquet flooring with an oil finish. Under-floor heating is to be accommodated where possible under hard finishes in the living area and bathrooms/en suites.

The Jeffries' home will be refurbished to a high-quality finish that can be easily maintained.

Rooms

Master bedroom, dressing room, en suite
Bedroom 1 with en suite
Bedroom 2 with en suite
Guest bedroom
Open-plan living area consisting of:

- *formal seating*
- *informal seating for television*
- *dining area for 8–10 people*
- *kitchen.*

Entrance hall with closet and storage
Guest WC
Laundry to be relocated off ground floor
Studio
Library

Interior Furnishings

The interior finishes and furnishings package will take into account the mix of classical and contemporary detail. Existing finishes sympathetic to the period of the building will be kept and restored, where necessary. Any new hard finishes will be of stone and wood and not imitation. Wallpapers will be included in most rooms. Furniture, lighting, and soft furnishings will be largely replaced, excepting a few sentimental pieces.

Refurbishment

The scope of the refurbishment will include the design and installation of all walls, floors, ceiling linings, new bathrooms, kitchen, fixed cupboards and joinery, electrics (to include rewiring where necessary, to incorporate new technology), lighting (replacing existing with LED, where possible), an updated security system and plumbing. The design will require the sympathetic retention of some listed items (to be determined) and the overall theme will be a mix of classic and contemporary detail and furnishing.

The following plans show the existing layout:

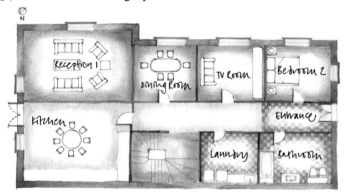

EXISTING GROUND FLOOR

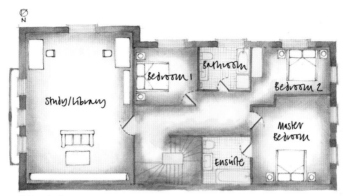

EXISTING FIRST FLOOR

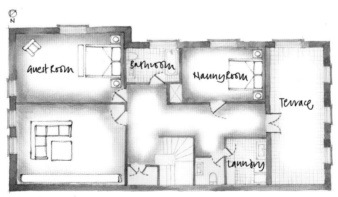

EXISTING SECOND FLOOR

MY 10 'DESIGN' STEPS

I have devised this 10-step design process to guide you into realising your boutique environment. It aims to introduce you to all facets of interior design, showing you what you need to take into consideration at each stage to provide you with the confidence and know-how to make informed decisions. Whether you undertake the project yourself or work with professionals will be your choice. However, I would advise you to know your own limits and when to hand over the decision-making to professionals. My wish is that this book will help you do that.

STEP 1: EVALUATING YOU
Recognise what you really want, clarify your brief and create a vision of your future.

Step 2: EVALUATING YOUR SPACE
Take the information from your brief and develop a list of what you require from your space.

Step 3: DESIGNING YOUR SPACE
Now plan your layout and consider the relationship of spaces and furniture.

STEP 4: CHOOSING YOUR COLOUR PALETTE
The world of colour is infinite; now's the time to plan colour into your scheme and devise a palette for your home.

STEP 5: SELECTING YOUR FINISHES
Make decisions based on appropriateness, practicality and aesthetics of hard and soft finishes.

STEP 6: SELECTING AND PLACING YOUR FURNITURE
What furniture should you keep? How and what to buy, taking into account appropriate size, comfort and aesthetics.

STEP 7: SELECTING YOUR SOFT FURNISHINGS
Develop a textural palette for your space, taking into account the overall scheme, palette and placement of texture and colour.

STEP 8: LIGHTING YOUR SPACE
Create a lighting scheme that is both practical and pleasing.

STEP 9: STYLING AND ACCESSORISING YOUR SPACE
Now add those touches that make your house a home and will enable you to express yourself through your collectables.

STEP 10: PLANNING YOUR WORK PROGRAMME
Finally, an outline and an overview of how to achieve and install your vision from beginning to end, what to communicate to trades and craftsmen, as well as what to look out for.

Before we begin THE FIVE MOST COMMON MISTAKES YOU WANT TO AVOID

Before we begin the journey step by step, let's take a moment to look at the five main mistakes that people make when designing their home.

We've all watched the magical transformations on DIY and makeover programmes, and felt convinced that, with a little flair, enthusiasm and muscle power, we too could achieve a dream interior. However, what we don't see behind the scenes is the fact that most of it is being held together with either double-sided tape or pins.

As a consequence of making rushed decisions on site, or making emotional decisions on buying trips, expensive and permanent mistakes can be made. The quick fix then ends up being the nightmare you have to live with or pay to rectify.

These are five of the most common mistakes:
- Failing to take the time to plan and lack of attention to detail
- Underestimating the amount of time and money a renovation project will take
- Underestimating the power of colour, pattern and texture
- Impulse buying and decision-making without thinking things through
- Not finishing the home with the right accessories and art.

Before you read through the steps in the book, it is a good idea to be realistic about these points.

FAILING TO TAKE THE TIME TO PLAN

The misconception that a quick fix will solve your lifestyle or space problems is the first of many mistakes. A lick of paint and a cosmetic makeover may achieve a temporary 'wow' factor but won't address the longer-term issues of planning for growth and comfort.

Take time to evaluate where you are now: what is and isn't comfortable, what you would like and how you would like to live in the space. This is essential to the success of creating a home to fit you and your family. Step 1 will help you work through the evaluation of what you want and where you would like to be. Step 2 will help you to evaluate how you would like to live in the space for the future.

Remember how much you enjoyed your holiday – its location and ambience. You researched the perfect hotel for your needs, in the right location, taking into account the cultural activities available. Taking time to evaluate what was best for your holiday needs was time well spent. This same thoughtful process is essential when designing a home to cater for your needs.

Many of us spend some 344 days of the year in the comfort and security of our homes. If comfort can be described on a physical and visual level, how *comfortable* are you? Think about the chair/sofa you are sitting in and the other pieces/elements in the room.

- Is the seating comfortable?
- Do you like the elements/pieces?
- Is the finished look expressing you?

You deserve to live in a space that expresses your lifestyle, your comfort and your taste – an environment that is tailored to your needs.

When you plan, you need to think of the future. Just think how much has changed in your own life in the past 12 months: relationships, career and health. When you plan with the flexibility of change and growth in mind you won't outgrow the space.

Attention to detail and viewpoints is critical. The placement of elements such as power points, dealing with awkward spaces and making the most of viewpoints such as garden or architectural features will all help to realise the value of the space.

UNDERESTIMATING THE AMOUNT OF TIME AND MONEY A RENOVATION PROJECT WILL TAKE

Generally, the first inclination when planning for a completion date is to choose a notable month or time, such as Christmas, as the deadline. However, with the best intentions in the world, this doesn't always happen – every project has its complexities in varying degrees. In Step 10, I have provided an outline of a job/project so you can anticipate what needs to be done. Your project will be dependent on its complexity in design and programming, issues such as planning and unforeseen problems with the building. We've all seen this happen on design TV programmes and is often led by the client changing the brief, which invariably adds more time, labour and therefore cost to the project. So it is a good idea to be prepared for eventualities that are beyond your control so as to avoid disappointment. Always allow for a contingency on projects. There will be inevitable increases in the budget due to delays and changes on the job, or price increases on materials, and so on.

In order to monitor this and be alert to any changes, work to a building programme with a project manager and contractor. Estimate with as much certainty as possible a feasible building works deadline, then maintain this by including penalties for any overrun in the contract.

UNDERESTIMATING THE POWER OF COLOUR, PATTERN AND TEXTURE

When most of us think colour, we may, for example, think red, yellow, blue, purple, orange or green, etc. But when we are working with colour, the full characteristics of **tone** and **saturation/purity** also need to be taken into account. The varying tones of colour can visually change the apparent size and proportions of a room. If darker tones are used in a scheme, it can make the space appear smaller. Conversely, lighter tones can make a room appear more spacious.

The warmth and coolness of colours can change the atmosphere and even the perceived temperature of a room. Consider how easy it is to choose the wrong white. It looked the perfect match from the paint fan, but in the room itself it appeared sullied or grey. You could choose a white with warm undertones for the cooler part of the house, or with cooler undertones for the warmer end of the house.

Variations in saturation and purity of a colour on furniture, objects and walls will effectively create contrast and add vitality to a scheme. However, it is important to consider the effect of warm colours that advance and cool colours that recede (discussed in 'Step 4, Choosing your colour palette').

Colour can't be seen without design. Select colour together with pattern and texture to enhance the core elements: architecture, furniture and atmosphere. Texture adds interest and works beautifully with the play of light to enhance form. Pattern can visually change the shape of the room – consider the effect of diagonal floor tiles in a galley kitchen.

IMPULSE BUYING AND DECISION-MAKING WITHOUT THINKING THINGS THROUGH

I'm sure that at some point you have bought an item of clothing on impulse and, once home, found it didn't match anything in your wardrobe. It was one of those moments when it felt so good and right, and you just had to have it! Before walking out of the shop or signing on the dotted line, it would be great if we could evaluate the reason for our choice before that sinking feeling overcomes us. Your home is one of the largest purchases you will make and therefore you need to make the right decision. You will be guided through this evaluation process for your home in Step 1.

If emotional decisions made on large items of furniture, finishes or structural items in the building are the wrong choices, then the change incurs cost on not just the product, but also on labour, and in turn causes delays. You can see the ramifications of this when the timetable has to be changed. And if it is too costly to change, the scheme, comfort and look of a space may be spoiled. The selection process for finishes, furniture and soft furnishings is discussed in Steps 5, 6 and 7.

You will also never make a decision again without considering **practicality**, **aesthetics** and **comfort**:

- **Practicality:** is the design practical for its purpose? Is the finish going to withstand the wear and tear of its intended use?
- **Aesthetics:** how does the design fit into the style and period of the building? Is the colour, shade, and texture of the material complementary to the scheme? How does size, visual weight and colour balance with other elements in the room?
- **Comfort:** how comfortable is an item of furniture or a space for its intended use? The value of comfort cannot be underestimated. A chair or layout that doesn't fulfil the requirements of its use will not only feel uncomfortable but look that way too.

NOT FINISHING THE HOME WITH THE RIGHT ACCESSORIES AND ART

In an interior your preferences for art, objects and artefacts, photographs and books is almost like the window to your soul. You are showing us who you are, what you like and where you have been. Your house needs these to become a home – think what a difference even a vase of fresh flowers makes in brightening up a dull atmosphere.

If you don't have a vast collection of items, or have unframed prints and photographs, now is the time to go shopping and introduce new pieces that will add the right personality to your home. Sift through what you already have; prints, photos and collectables from your travels can be collated and displayed in groupings that are in keeping with the style and atmosphere of your room. In this way, you will be unveiling some of your history and introducing new items that represent you now.

I'll be discussing how to arrange your collection in Step 9.

Let us now begin the design process with 'Evaluating you', covered in Step 1.

Step 1 EVALUATING YOU

When you invite friends into your home, you are showing them who you are, what you like and how you live. **Your space is your statement to the world.** They will experience the layout of space, the impact of the colour scheme and the quality of the textures and finishes you have chosen. What you have created in your space, the items you have collected and the furniture you have chosen all signify the way you wish to live and the things you enjoy living with. So is your space authentic to you?

If not, let's create your vision.

There are two key elements that form the driving force behind achieving the look and feel you want:
- Encapsulating your lifestyle in words – 5–6 adjectives.
- Encapsulating your style and the ambience you would like in pictures – a **mood board**.

Working through this process helps you to:
- clarify the lifestyle you want; and
- visualise your dream home.

This in turn will make your choices easier in the design and selection process.

INVESTING IN YOURSELF

I think it was Kevin McCloud (presenter of the TV programme, *Grand Designs*) who said, '… a building should reflect the best of people and place…' And so, too, should the interior. Whether you are in a space for two months or 20 years, you should feel uplifted and nurtured in your surroundings. Let your space be authentic and express YOU!

Research has shown that our immediate environment affects our behaviour. It is your choice to live in an environment that speaks of your aspirations, your taste and your lifestyle. Once you have made the decision to change, to re-establish your focus and to implement a new design, the effect can also be transformational to your behaviour. And, if we create an environment that nurtures we too will feel nurtured.

When I first visit the home of a potential client, I am aware that the space may need decorative and/or structural changes. The changes necessary and the extent of the work proposed are made to fulfil the new requirements of the owner.

Some previous clients of mine recently moved to Singapore from Australia for 18 months. Having moved from a beautiful lifestyle home, they were now renting a large, but rather bland, house. The furniture came with it – acceptable but not suited to their taste or comfort. They accepted it all as a short-term contract and refused to spend 'dead money' on a home they didn't own. At the end of the 18-month contract, the husband was offered a substantial pay increase to extend his contract to three years. This was a great opportunity, but they felt reticent about accepting, given the lovely home they had left in Australia.

I advised my clients to make decorative changes to the space to express their tastes, and to replace furniture with pieces they liked that felt physically comfortable and could then be added to their scheme at home in Australia. I believe that, whether you are renting or buying, the space where you live is home. They re-negotiated with the landlord to re-paint and decorate, and to empty the flat of existing furniture, and began filling it with things they loved. This change of attitude led to changing their lifestyle and entertaining as they would have done in Australia. Consequently, they turned their house into a home and turned the quality of their life around in the process.

Interior design is an investment and, whether decorative or structural, it will affect the quality of your life. The quality of the investment not only increases the value of your property, it is an **investment in you** and your psychological wellbeing.

HOW TO VALUE YOURSELF AND DEFINE YOUR LIFESTYLE

As you create a space that reflects you, watch your lifestyle change. Reviving and manipulating the spaces within your home, revamping or replacing fixtures and furniture, and displaying and lighting objects/art, will give it a new lease of life and make you feel more comforted by the space.

Take the time to complete the following exercise, reflecting on your lifestyle and answering the questions outlined below about where you are now and how you would like to live. It's your time to express and evaluate what you really want. Alongside this exercise, I will be following our case study, the Jeffries family, so we can see how they begin to define their vision.

DEFINING YOUR REQUIREMENTS AND STYLE

What are your living requirements?

Consider how you are living now and how you would really like to be living in the future. Is the way you use your home likely to stay the same or change? Will you have family members moving in or out? Addressing any changes like these will help with the overall proposed layout and zoning of areas.

The Jeffries' children still live at home and both Sally and Peter have growing interests and hobbies – art and book collecting as well as furniture restoration.

What is your lifestyle (as a family)?

This includes sports and leisure activities for all the family. You want to make sure there is enough storage and that it is in a convenient and accessible space.

The Jeffries have accumulated bikes, skis and tennis rackets over the years. They would like to consolidate these into one space that is accessible and well organised.

How do you like to entertain and for how many?

Perhaps you like to cook and/or there may be a requirement for formal entertaining. This will influence the size of kitchen, the white goods necessary (i.e. oven, fridge, dishwasher) and its access to dining areas indoors and outdoors.

The Jeffries need to entertain both professionally and socially. They will possibly entertain business guests once a month, sitting six guests in the more formal seating area and at the dining table. As a family, they enjoy conversation and eating. This may include one or two of their friends or children's friends. They like to cook simply, with local and farm produce. They would also like the flexibility of indoor and outdoor entertaining.

Your indoor activities – how do you want to use the space?

This evaluates the connection of spaces. For example, dining to kitchen or master bedroom to en suite. Do you have the room to expand? You may have to extend up or out, which may involve planning restrictions. There is always room somewhere – the current trend is for subterranean development, which creates space underground, adding more square footage and therefore more value to the house.

The Jeffries want more privacy and space for the family bedrooms. They would also like the guest bedroom to be on a separate level away from the living areas.

How does each room work?
By evaluating the activities for each room you can make sure that you have the space, the storage and the equipment needed, e.g. the kitchen could be zoned for breakfast, coffee/tea making, baking, washing, preparation, cooking, eating, service dishes, cutlery and cool and dry storage.

For the Jeffries family, the kitchen is the hub of the house. They enjoy cooking simply with fresh ingredients and eating together as a family.

At what time of the day do you use each room?
Knowing this defines how a space can be used at night and during the day.

As Sally works from home she would like her studio to have an outlook and good natural light. As a family they enjoy watching films, mostly at night.

How comfortable are you in your space?
- Does your bedroom offer you the right kind of comfort, privacy and relaxation? What would improve it?
- How comfortable is your living room? Is it relaxing and in a style you are happy with? What would make it more comfortable?
- How well does the space work in your kitchen? Is it pleasant to cook and eat in? What would make it better?
- How comfortable is your bathroom? Does it feel as luxurious as you would like? What would make it more relaxing?
- How impressive is your entrance?
- What would make it more attractive and welcoming?

The comfort of materials underfoot was a requirement for the Jeffries. They have requested that wood flooring replace carpets for ease of maintenance and comfort in the living areas. They would also like underfloor heating in all bathrooms.

What is your personal style?

Your personal style is an expression of you now so if it feels out of date consider ways within your budget to update.

The Jeffries want a style that expresses a casual sophistication with the integrity of natural materials, i.e. stone and wood.

How technologically friendly is your home and how would you like it to be?

Do you want everything controlled at the touch of a button, and from the arm of your sofa? It is a personal choice but one that needs to be considered early on in the planning and building of your space.

The Jeffries need a system that will allow sound, heat and light to be controlled remotely. They would also like the curtains and blinds incorporated, depending on cost. Security is key to the upgrade of the house. All access will be via intercom, and the lighting in both front and back gardens will need to be controlled on a sensory basis.

Your colour preferences

What colours do you enjoy or dislike living with? Colour is the first thing we see and react to when entering a room so make the right choice.

Think of the aspect: does your room face north or south? For example, how cold or warm is the room, how large or small is it and what activities take place in it? There will be more on this in 'Step 4, Choosing your colour palette'. Don't be too caught up in trends, as they will come and go; the seemingly elegant taupe interiors of today will no doubt be the drab of tomorrow.

The Jeffries are not afraid of bold statements. The rooms receive plenty of natural light and they don't want to lose this.

YOUR VISUAL STATEMENT

Defining your style with key adjectives
At this early stage, let's for the moment forget the budget and practicalities and concentrate on the mood, the setting and your lifestyle.

You want to create an environment that expresses your taste and lifestyle. The mood you create will convey the tone, texture, vitality and lightness or darkness of the space – its ambience.

To help you clarify your thinking, describe your lifestyle and the mood it suggests, encapsulating the mood in adjectives.

The Jeffries family chose these adjectives to describe their ideal interior:
- *natural*
- *textural*
- *casual sophistication*
- *expressive*
- *classic/contemporary with an element of surprise.*

Review your brief, highlighting words that evoke the mood or setting and depict your lifestyle. You will notice that certain points and words will stand out to suggest an atmosphere or function of the environment. For example, 'open-plan living' correlates to the word **spacious**. You may also have suggested a connection between the 'indoor and outdoor' environment, which could suggest a **natural** setting. Also, **texture** may be a key element you would like in your space, or **light, spacious, airy**, or **urban, cutting edge, dynamic**.

Notice a theme beginning to emerge from the four or five adjectives used, which will reveal a lifestyle statement. Remember that this represents the essence of the space or atmosphere you are trying to capture. Most importantly, these adjectives must ring true to you and your lifestyle.

For example:
- cool, fresh, light, spacious, casual
- sleek, urban, avant-garde, cutting edge
- textural, natural, fresh, casual, organic
- rich, sumptuous, elegant, textural.

Express your lifestyle in pictures – make a mood board
The mood or concept board interprets the adjectives into pictures and will be your visual tool of reference. It will help you make decisions on planning, detailing and the selection of finishes, furniture and accessories. The mood could be reflected in the design layout: spacious and light, or perhaps organic. The colour scheme will also be influenced by the mood board.

How to make your own mood board

1. From a collection of magazines choose images that reflect the adjectives/your lifestyle. These images do not need to be room sets, they could be sections of line, texture or space that show the energy and vitality of the space you would like.
2. Find the colour, texture or sculptural quality and line that will convey your message. This doesn't have to come from an interior shot; there may be elements of nature that show the form and texture you seek. Or it may be a room section depicting the light, space or elements that you would like to introduce.
3. Once you have collated a selection of images, you can present them in either digital or paper format. Lay out the images in an arrangement that reflects the mood and dynamics of the atmosphere. It is easier to work from the centre of the page outwards.
4. The object of the exercise is to create a visual statement that matches your descriptive adjectives. Remember that often '**less is more**'. Try to choose large images for visual impact.
5. Glue the images to the board, or transfer the jpegs into a creative software format such as Adobe InDesign.

The mood board you have now created is your tool of reference for the design process and sourcing trips to choose products. It's a good idea to take a picture of your mood board on your mobile phone so that you have it as a reference.

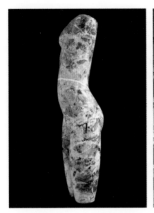

This is the mood board for the Jeffries' living space; casual sophistication with the all-important element of surprise (see www.interiorstatements.co.uk for other examples of mood boards).

MY SEVEN TOP TIPS FOR EVALUATING YOUR STYLE

Decide to live in a home that is authentic to you.

- ▶ Clarify what you want.
- ▶ Define your style.
- ▶ Review your existing space.
- ▶ Define your requirements.
- ▶ Express your lifestyle in pictures.
- ▶ Define what colour scheme you would like.

You have now set the tone and style of your home. You have focused on the two elements: your adjectives describing your space and your mood board expressing what you would like in pictures.

You are now in a position to define what you really need from your physical space. This leads you into 'Step 2, Evaluating your space'.

Step 2

EVALUATING YOUR SPACE

 EVALUATING YOUR SPACE

Now that you have evaluated just what you want, it's time to evaluate your space – does your home as it is now fit the requirements of your lifestyle? This step helps you define what you need from your spaces/rooms – the **purpose**, **function** and **ambience** required within each room.

DEFINING YOUR SPACES

The spaces within your home can generally be divided into **public** and **private** areas:
- **Public** – the spaces we all use: entrance, hallways, kitchen, dining and living areas
- **Private** – the quieter areas such as bedrooms and attached bathrooms.

The rooms within these areas have general and specific requirements, as outlined below.

PUBLIC AREAS

Entrance: Your home's first impression – it requires a welcoming atmosphere, good visibility and durable finishes, particularly on the floor.

Kitchen: This is often the hub of the house – considerations include:
- Who will cook and for how many?
- The style of cooking (some cultural foods have a strong aroma), which in turn will call for good ventilation.

Dining room: Whether formal or more casual, the emphasis is bringing together people to enjoy food and company. Take into account how many people will be dining and whether storage and space for setting down platters of food is required.

Living room: Decide whether this is a formal or casual room. Consider:
- Your focal points.
- How many people need to be seated.
- What activities will be involved and at what times of the day.
- Lighting and how central lamps will be wired in.

Office/study: Decide how many people will be using this space, at what time of the day and what storage is required. What technology will be required? What equipment will need to be housed and how will it be wired in?

Games/ cinema room: This is the leisure entertainment space – movies and games. In open-plan spaces this is often a part of the living room.

Conservatory: This space is treated as a garden room where light and external viewpoints are the strong points. Make sure this space is heated, whether by underfloor, radiators or a fire, so the space can be used year round. Insulate glass to reflect the heat in summer and retain it during the winter.

PRIVATE AREAS

Master bedroom: This is a space of retreat and sanctuary. Zone the room so it can be used for sleeping, relaxing and reading. Design the lighting around these zones for tasks and indirect mood lighting. As the bed is normally the focal point in the bedroom, the size and style of the bed will dictate the theme of the room.

Master en suite: Decide what you require: bath, WC, bidet, double basins, shaving points, a mirror, underfloor heating and whether you want the space to be a wet room.

Dressing room/ wardrobe: Take into account how much space you will require for clothes (hanging space and shelves/drawers), shoes, and bags.

Guest room: Think of how you want your guests to feel in your home, and the conveniences they need: hanging, shelving space and luggage storage, bench space. If this room needs to be used for storage of other items, design built-in furniture to house it.

Guest en suite: Decide what the essentials are – a good size shower may be better than trying to squeeze in a bath as well. A good amount of layoff space and shelves will be useful.

Study-tech area: Plan for computers and a desk area as well as shelving for books and folders.

External: The garden is an extension of the home and can be zoned to take into account dining and lounging.

SURVEYING YOUR EXISTING SPACE

In order to evaluate what you need from a space, you will now need to survey *what is existing.* This takes into account critical dimensions and relevant notes on the condition of the elements in each room.

You will need to record information on the existing condition, size and detail of each room. This will enable you to:

- **Evaluate** the room's current use.
- **Ascertain** whether the use needs to be changed.
- **Consider** how else it could be used.

For the survey, be equipped with notepad, pen, steel measuring tape and camera. Sketch a plan (an example is below) and record dimensions of the room size, heights of ceilings, doors, windows, and the placement of power sockets. You will be taking notes and photos for your reference.

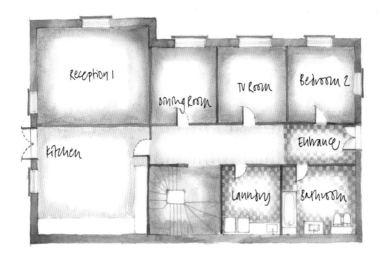

Once you have surveyed the room, you can then decide **which elements you wish to keep, remove or refurbish**.

EVALUATING THE EXISTING SPACE

Think carefully about structural changes. Look at your physical parameters and review the **best** and **worst** of each space. You want to get it right the first time – once an element is removed it isn't easy or cheap to replace it.

To evaluate each space, you will need to consider the following:

The best and the worst features:
- Take note of the **best** features in the room – those you want to keep.
- Then, take note of the **worst** features in the room – those to be removed or concealed. This may be exposed pipe work.

Decorative condition of the space:
- What is the overall condition of the space?
- Will it need to be decorated, re-plastered?
- Is there any damp, or other issues to make good?

Height of the room:
- Is the ceiling unusually low or high?

Shape of the room:
- Is the shape rectangular, square or uneven?
- Is the room lacking good proportion?

Shape and placement of the windows:
- Do the windows enhance the space?
- Is there enough daylight?
- What are the external viewpoints from the windows?

Doors:
- Will the doors need replacing or refurbishing?
- Can the door opening be widened?
- Is the door furniture worth saving?

Flooring:
- What condition is the existing flooring?
- Is it repairable?
- Does it need to be replaced?

Walls:
- What is the general condition of the walls?
- Are there any elements of architectural interest?
- Are there any cracks that will need filling?
- Is there any structural damage?

Ceiling:
- Does the coving or ceiling rose need to be replaced or refurbished?
- Are there any cracks or structural damage to the ceiling?

Lighting and electrics:
- What is the existing lighting in the room?
- Is this in good repair?
- Will it need replacing?
- How many power sockets are there?
- Will these need replacing to conform with new regulations?

Heating:
- What is the condition of radiators or underfloor heating?
- Will they need refurbishing?

Kitchen units:
- Are the kitchen cabinets in good condition?
- Will they need replacing ?

Bathroom suites:
- Will all or some of the bathroom fixtures need replacing?
- Will the ventilation need replacing?

Built-in cabinetry and wardrobes:
- Take note of the condition and value to your scheme
- Will the wardrobes need to be removed or replaced?

THE USE OF EACH SPACE

Even if you have plans to expand the size of your home, making the best use of your spaces so they work for you is what matters.

Existing use:
- What is the space currently being used for? For the most part this is obvious, but with a full description of each room there may be overlaps or questions as to why a task is performed in that particular room
- What are the problems with the existing space?
- Evaluate the task and where it is performed, and at what times of the day.

Proposed use of space:
- How would you like to use the space?
- Can the room have a change of use?
- For example, often the existing kitchen space will be incorporated into the living space in new layouts.

Your requirements for the space:
- What are the key items required in the space? These could include fixtures and fittings, such as fridges and dishwashers for a kitchen, or large loose furniture such as beds, sofas etc.

Storage:
- What storage is required? Storage is an issue in many apartments and houses designed today. As space is at a premium price per square foot, look at all available 'dead' space as potential storage.

Below is the existing ground floor plan for the Jeffries' reception/kitchen areas.

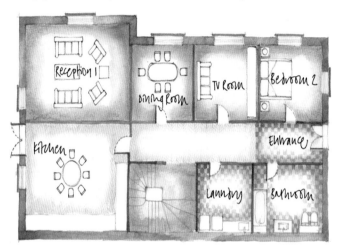

To help you remember all the details as you survey your space, you can draw up a list in a table like the one below.

THE JEFFRIES' SURVEY OF RECEPTION 1

Physical elements	Description/condition	Comments
Fireplace	Good	Mantle needs replacing
Built-in furniture	Poor	To be removed
Height of room	Approx. 3.5 m	
Shape of room	Not very wide	Width to be emphasised

Physical elements	Description/condition	Comments
Shape & placement of windows	French doors	Need refurbishment
Doors internal	Poor	Sand and re-paint
Flooring	Carpet	Floorboards to be revealed and oiled
Walls	Papered	Replace wallpaper Re-paint dado/picture rail
Ceiling	Rose missing Cracks	Replace rose Fill/make good
Fixtures & fittings		
Chandelier	Missing lights	Clean/replace bulbs
Downlights	Poorly designed layout	Replace with wall washers
Power points	Plastic	Replace with satin brass
Phone points	Not included	Replace with computer/phone access
Low radiator under window	Good	Re-paint & house
Use of space		
Existing use		
Reception I	Formal	Entertaining guests
Reception 2	Informal	Family use

(continued on next page)

(continued from previous page)

Physical elements	Description/condition	Comments
Problems with space		
Reception 1	Little light during day	Needs light to compensate
Reception 2	Good daylight	Needs blackout for TV screening
Preferred use of space		
Reception 2	To replace reception 1	Locate closer to kitchen
Key items required in space		
Reception 2 – living	To be multifunctional	TV – 42 in Update technology
Required storage		Storage of CDs and DVDs, games
Book storage		New, bespoke item

MY SEVEN TOP TIPS FOR EVALUATING YOUR SPACE

- Survey each room, sketching plan and elevations.
- Photograph each room.
- Note the best and worst features.
- Note the use of each space.
- Note the existing problems.
- Note what you want from the space.
- Note the key items you require.

This process is worth the time and effort, as this evaluation will have a large impact on the design and spatial layout of rooms. You have considered the **physical parameters** of your space, the **fixtures and fittings** and the **use of your space,** which is essential information to proceed to the next phase, 'Step 3, Designing your space'.

 # Step 3 DESIGNING YOUR SPACE

Once you have:
- clarified your brief
- created a mood board and
- evaluated your space

you now have the tools of reference to design the layout. Whether you trace the plan of a room or house, or can work on a computer, you will need dimensions of furniture, new and existing, to layout in plan format. Within the existing perimeter of the house you can re-arrange rooms to suit your needs and/or realise that an extension may need to be added.

The planning will address:
- your lifestyle objectives;
- the ideal relationship between spaces;
- the activities and purpose of each room;
- flexibility for growth; and
- technology.

You need to consider what best fits *your* lifestyle, not just what is trendy or fashionable. After all, we may not all want to be living with glass walls, high-gloss kitchens and uber-sophisticated technology systems. Your home needs to fit your needs and personality. Of course, respecting the period of the building and its character goes without saying – do think again before ripping out history. Thankfully, our buildings are mostly protected from reckless renovations on the outside.

THE DESIGN SOLUTION

Space planning
This will affect the shape and size of the spaces, so remember to:
- Plan a layout inclusive of all items of furniture, built-in and free-standing, fixtures, finishes, and, of course, lighting.
- Optimise and allow natural light to filter through the room spaces
- size the space to suit the purpose. Walls may have to be removed to create the open space and structural support required as a consequence.
- Take advantage of viewpoints, internally and externally, to visually extend your space. One of the current design trends is to replace the back wall of the house with glass windows that either slide or concertina. In this way the indoor space is integrated with the outdoors and in good weather can double the size of entertaining space.
- Plan for the future so you can grow into the space.

THE JEFFRIES' NEW GROUND FLOOR LAYOUT

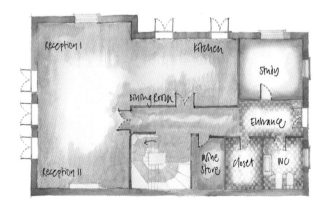

The Jeffries' proposed ground floor layout has connected the reception rooms with the kitchen and dining area, creating an L-shaped open-plan layout and a more integrated lifestyle. Existing windows have been replaced with French doors in the dining/kitchen areas, integrating indoors/outdoors. The Jeffries like open-plan living so have incorporated the existing TV room as part of this space. The removal of the adjoining wall meant structural support was necessary, achieved by installing a metal RSJ beam. (Check with a structural engineer before removing walls, particularly in basement flats.)

THE JEFFRIES' NEW FIRST FLOOR LAYOUT

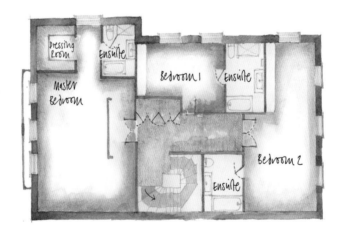

The Jeffries' proposed first floor layout has relocated the master bedroom to the north-west corner, incorporating dressing room and en suite. Both bedroom 1 and 2 have been enlarged to include more storage and en suites. The layout provides more space, storage and privacy for all bedrooms.

THE JEFFRIES' NEW SECOND FLOOR LAYOUT

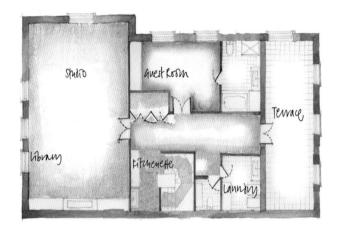

The Jeffries' proposed second floor layout creates a separated guest room and en suite with kitchenette. A large studio/library space has also been incorporated on this level with the light and privacy required. The laundry room has also been housed upstairs to connect with the bedrooms and terrace area.

FEATURES, FIXTURES AND FOCAL POINTS TO CONSIDER

Respecting the period of the building

If you have a period property and need to extend your house, do your research. Make sure you work with an architect who has experience of period properties to ensure that any transitional details between the old and new are sympathetic and that your lifestyle and storage is catered for.

Step 3

The best and worst features of your rooms

Once the use of each space is clarified you will need to consider your focal points.

- The **best features** in a room can be architectural elements such as fireplaces, architraves/cornices, or it may be the size or the height of the room. Look for natural focal points as a key grounding point for the room. Stairs are also a natural focal point in many entrance halls. You may be able to highlight the sculptural form of the stair and/or detail of the banister, tread or newel.
- The **worst** features in the room may be additions that can be removed, existing pipe work that could be boxed in and concealed, or it may be that the space is small with low ceilings. All of these elements will need to be addressed in the design planning to make the most of the space.

Assessing fixtures – to replace, re-site or remove

Do the existing built-in wardrobes, bathroom suites, kitchen cabinets, radiators and lighting work with your scheme, practically and aesthetically?

Assess the need to re-site or replace items such as boilers and radiators so that they can be plumbed in.

Specifying your technology

Just how much or how little technology you wish to design into the scheme will be driven by your requirements and budget. If you want all-singing and -dancing technology that opens curtains, creates mood lighting, accesses music and films and provides security from the touch of a button, make sure you plan this in from the beginning. Control motors and operation hubs will need to be accommodated and cleverly concealed. Trying to integrate this at the end of the project will inevitably cost and may not be achievable.

Designing adequate storage

Adequate and convenient storage will clean up visual clutter and create order within your environment.

Having evaluated your requirements for storage, plan it into the build from the beginning to avoid any expensive re-design at a later date. Clever storage can be concealed within the fabric of the building or designed into furniture as a bespoke item. Look at all options – you can never have enough storage.

DEALING WITH PROPORTION

Height of the room

If the room height needs to be increased to create the illusion of space, visually emphasise the vertical line and choose focal points that are placed low in the room. Conversely, if the room needs to be reduced in height, emphasise the horizontal line and select height lines well below the ceiling height.

Shape of the room

If the room is too small, too large or oddly shaped:

- Apply colour to focal points to change the emphasis of the existing shape.
- Add decorative or architectural elements to enhance height or width.
- Use lighting to emphasise and deflect.
- Group furniture to define circulation paths.

Shape and placement of windows

If the shape of the windows is not in proportion with the room, or if there isn't enough natural light, consider how the window can be either altered structurally or visually enlarged with decorative window treatment; for example, by placing the curtain pole nearer to the cornice rather than on the window architrave will visually heighten the room.

Front door

As the front door is the first impression of your home, it will need to make the right statement. Ideally, the door should retain the period of the building (as viewed from the outside) and set the tone for what lies beyond.

If the door needs replacing, question the existing size of the opening. Look for other height lines to align the door to, such as the top of the window. Opting for oversized doors can increase the visual height of the room, but remember to retain this cohesion throughout. The design and finish of your internal doors should complement your scheme. The choice of finish and detail of hardware will suggest the quality of the internal space. The door furniture items on the market today are statement pieces, so choose wisely, combining the period of the property and harmony with your scheme.

Flooring

Floors will be one of the most important and expensive elements in your scheme, and will set **tone** and **mood.** We will look at flooring in more detail in Step 5.

Often the building will have an existing floor that fits the period and style of the building and is worthy of restoration. It is a significant factor in the historical value of the building, so don't dismiss what is already there. Retaining historical elements connects the past to the present.

For example, during the refurbishment of what was historically a Victorian factory, we wanted to retain every period detail. As the building's history was one of industrial and commercial use, any redeeming architectural features needed restorative work. The existing flooring had been painted with six to seven layers of paint, which we stripped and stained to match the grey-stained oak in the new areas of the building. This created a seamless transition between old and new flooring.

The selection process of your flooring material will need to take into account:

- **Aesthetics** – the colour, texture and design.
- **Appropriateness** – this relates to the building and activity of the room.
- **Maintenance** – the type of care required to keep it looking good and lasting.

Walls

Decide if any existing period detail is of architectural merit and complementary to your scheme. If not, colour, textural wallpapers, veneers, leather and mirror can all be applied to add focal points or backdrops to support your scheme.

With any finishing process good quality preparatory work is essential. A good decorator knows that walls need to be sanded down to erase any imperfections before application. This is particularly important for lacquered or glazed finishes or wallpaper. Advise the decorators as to whether you will need lining paper on the walls, and always follow hanging instructions as some wallpapers, such as silk, do not adhere well to lined walls.

A good point to remember: if you have specified luxury finishes, wallpapers and unusual finishes, make sure your trades people have worked with these finishes before.

Ceiling

If the existing ceiling is being retained, list which areas need to be 'made good' (i.e. restored) and which need to be replaced and/or removed.

The lighting and electrical layout of a room will be planned once the furniture layout has been planned and confirmed. The ceiling will therefore need to be prepared for any new fittings. We will look at lighting in more detail in Step 8.

Zoning for a furniture layout

Zoning is generally based around seating areas, particularly in open-plan spaces. Having more than one seating area adds interest to the space. Try to create space for circulation between the zones, which adds to the comfort but also visually organises the space. Once the zones are allocated, then decide what furniture is required and how many people will need to use it, for example seating areas.

As you allocate furniture to the zones, use it as a time to review each piece with your mood board – does it fit into the atmosphere and tone of the scheme? Does the furniture arrangement fit within the zone and consider circulation space? Is the visual weight of the furniture in keeping with the atmosphere?

At the end of the process, if you have chosen with clarity and consideration, your selection will not only be pleasing to the eye but very comfortable to live with.

CASE STUDY: THE JEFFRIES' PARAMETERS IN DESIGNING

The consideration of existing period elements was an important issue to the Jeffries' project as they did not want the new layout to lose the history of the building.

The fireplace would have to be restored, but the flooring had to be replaced as the combination of flooring between the rooms needed to be seamless and practical in both kitchen and living areas. They chose oil-finished, engineered parquet flooring as a warm, clean finish that was also appropriate to the period of the building.

The windows in the proposed kitchen and dining areas were replaced with French doors, taking into account conservation regulations of triple glazing and materials.

The ceiling had to be made good and cornicing replaced where walls had been removed.

MY SEVEN TOP TIPS FOR DESIGNING YOUR SPACE

- Be sympathetic to the building and its history.
- Plan the layout to incorporate your needs.
- Design around focal points.
- Design to disguise less appealing elements.
- Zone your space to suit your lifestyle.
- Revamp or replace where necessary.
- Make sure your trades know how to install your product and finishes.

From this, you can now progress to extracting a **colour palette,** described in Step 4.

Step 4

CHOOSING YOUR
COLOUR PALETTE

Step 4 CHOOSING YOUR COLOUR PALETTE

Creating the colour scheme for a project holds both the excitement of colour and the challenge of making the right choice. The reason I spend time working to get this right is to make sure that the choice of finishes and colour creates the atmosphere that suits my client and their preferences.

Colour is the first thing we see when entering a space, so we want to choose a colour scheme that we feel uplifted by and at the same time will suit the purpose and function of the room.

You must recognise what the driving force behind your scheme is. Will it be influenced by existing elements such as art or an existing sofa/chair, or are you starting off with a clean slate?

You also need to know how colour can be made up of other hues, making it **warmer, colder, lighter, brighter** or **darker**:
- Mixing a cold hue like blue with hints of a warm hue like red will result in a warmer blue.
- Mixing hues with white will create lightness
- Mixing hues with black will create greater darkness.

This is a helpful tool to visually change proportion and change the mood of a room.

It is also important that colour samples are viewed on-site in the room you will be applying it to, taking into account the proposed lighting conditions. The diagrams in the 'Hues, tones, shades and tints' section will help you.

You need to know the correct placement and quantity of a particular colour, as well as tonal variation, to create the character of the scheme.

USING COLOUR IN YOUR SPACE

In order to make the right decision about colour choices, let's consider the following:

Your colour brief
When developing a scheme you will need to consider:
- culture;
- climate;
- the type of space – domestic, workplace, public space, safety zone, and/or retail space;
- features you would like to enhance in the space; and
- features you would like to minimise in the space.

The function and placement of colour
When working with colour, take into consideration its **function** within the room.

Is it being used to reflect light or is it a focal point? To reflect light, it will need to be a tint or brighter colour. As a focal piece it will need to be a bright or contrasting colour.

The **placement** of colour will be key to introducing focal points, character and atmosphere:
- If you want an element of furniture to stand out, contrast it to the background.
- If you want an element to be played down, approximate its colour and tone to the other elements or background.

Aspect
You can change the visual aspect of a room with colour. As described above, most colours have traces of other hues in their composition. For example, adding a blue tinge to white will make it feel colder, whereas hints of yellow or red will make it feel warmer or rosier. Therefore, it would be wiser to choose a warmer white for the colder end of your house.

Changing the proportion of your room

If you have a room that you would like to be more cosy or give the illusion of space, then:

- Use lighter tones to give the illusion of space.
- Use dark, rich or brighter tones to create more intimacy, give visual weight to the room or make it appear smaller.

Matching finishes

To **colour match** the white (as an example), you will need to match the undertone colour – knowing this will help you match other finishes to it. For example, if there is a greenish undertone to the white, match your finishes, such as the white kitchen worktop, to suit. There is a vast difference between brilliant white and stone white.

The balance of colour

Many of us underestimate the power and effect of colour. Have you noticed how sample paint always appears different once it is painted on the wall? This is because when painted en masse, the colour intensifies – sometimes by up to 50%. And if you add a bold design to the colour it is intensified further. Dark colours in a small room can produce a claustrophobic box unless relieved with lighter contrasts. Which in turn can be interesting and dramatic.

So, colour is your tool to emphasise or play down the various elements within a room.

It takes courage to carry this through as it is not until everything else goes back into the room that the drama unfolds. I remember my first bold experiment with colour in a kitchen, painting walls and cupboards a battleship grey. The initial effect was military, but once the sparkle of cupboard handles, crockery and accessories were placed into the room it took on an entirely new life.

Finally, once you have chosen the colour scheme think about the proportion of colour and which hue you would like to dominate in the scheme. This will create more visual balance than apportioning 50% of each colour.

WHAT YOU NEED TO KNOW ABOUT COLOUR

The most valuable tool for a designer is the colour wheel:

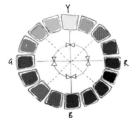

When using colour we recognise:

- its **hue,** i.e. colour name, for example red;
- its **value,** i.e. how much white or black is in the colour;
- **tints,** where a colour has been lightened with white;
- **shades,** created by mixing black and pure colour;
- **tones,** created by mixing grey and pure colours; and
- **intensity,** i.e. the degree of purity/saturation.

HUES, TONES/SHADES AND TINTS

If you look at the colour wheels below, you will notice that they all have the hues in the same arrangement but are different in saturation, tone/shade and tint.

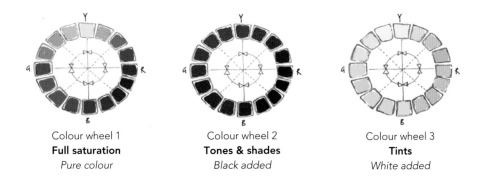

Colour wheel 1
Full saturation
Pure colour

Colour wheel 2
Tones & shades
Black added

Colour wheel 3
Tints
White added

Step 4

Tints and shades create variety and atmosphere in your scheme.

Generally:
- Lighter tints of colour will reflect light and make a room feel more spacious.
- Deeper shades of colour will make a room heavier and more cosy.
- Full saturation of colours will bring more activity and drama to a space.
- The warmer or darker a colour, the more it will advance, while the cooler, lighter colours will recede.
- Warm (red, orange and yellow) and saturated hues and dark tones advance, and therefore make an object look nearer and larger.
- Cool (green, blue and violet) and less saturated hues and light tones recede, and therefore make an object appear further away and smaller.

When you understand how to place and use colour with tone you can then transform the balance and character of a room:
- If a scheme is too bold, add mid-tones or neutrals to relieve the heaviness or starkness.
- To make a large colour palette work, use a smaller band of tones to reduce the visual energy of the colours.
- If a room doesn't have any architectural features, add slightly darker contrasts of tone into the scheme to add some vitality and create interest.

COLOUR SCHEMING AND PLANNING

All colour schemes are based around the following colours and their variants. From the colour spectrum/wheel and its various tints and shades we can formulate tried and tested schemes in order to create palettes and bring energy to a room. These schemes are helpful in order to create passive, harmonious or dynamic interiors.

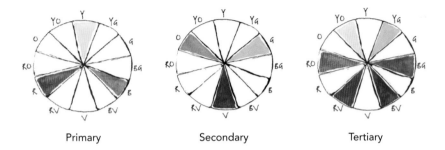

Primary   Secondary   Tertiary

The monochromatic scheme

Using just one colour in various tints and shades will emphasise form, line and texture. Architects such as Corbusier adored the effects of grey on grey to do just this.

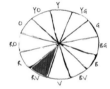

The analagous scheme

The colours selected are adjacent to each other on the wheel; for example, green, green-yellow and yellow. As they are closely related it produces a generally quiet scheme with little energy.

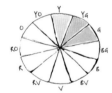

Contrasting/complementary scheming

By using two colours from the opposite side of the colour wheel, for example violet/yellow, or red/green, you can create a **complementary** scheme. This involves balancing opposites and is known to be the easiest scheme to live with.

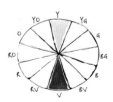

Step 4

Always take into account the brightness of each colour and the proportion needed to create the right balance. Usually, a small amount of yellow is needed to balance a violet-yellow scheme.

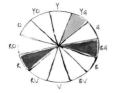

Split complementary
This expands the palette of a complementary scheme through the addition of a third colour. Use each colour either side of its opposite. For example, red, yellow/green, blue/green, or yellow, blue/violet, red violet.

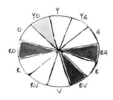

Double split complementary
This expands the scheme to four colours, using the two colours each side of the opposite colour at both ends of the wheel – for example, yellow/orange, red/orange and blue/violet, blue/green. When using a number of colours, you may need to keep the tonal band narrow, otherwise there may be clashes.

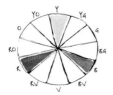

The triadic scheme
Each colour is equidistant to the other on the colour wheel, which creates a lot of energy. This can often be seen in children's play areas, using red, yellow and blue in full saturation.

THE MEANING AND IMPACT OF COLOUR

As a general rule:
- Red, orange and yellow are the most vigorous/energetic of hues.
- Blue, blue-green and violet are more passive, cold/cooling.

 Red is from the warm side of the colour wheel. It is bright, warm and advancing – great for showing off objects/furniture. Depending on the undertone red can be either stimulating or relaxing.

 Pink is the feminine, more nurturing tone of red. It can physically relax and calm the emotions. It's also a colour that takes the seriousness out of the atmosphere. I think dentists should use more of it!

 Orange mixes red (physical) and yellow (mental). It also adds a social element to the space and enhances the appetite – great as an accent in heavy dark spaces and used boldly.

 Yellow relates to the emotions and appears brighter than white – great used in dark spaces where there isn't much daylight.

 Green is made up of yellow (active) and blue (passive) – a yellow/green stimulates, a blue/green pacifies. As it sits midway between the warm and cool hues on the colour wheel, it relates to balance as well as nature.

 Blue is from the cool side of the wheel and has a receding effect. Depending on its composition, one can perceive it as a cooler or warmer blue.

 Purple can be viewed as **violet** – the red form of purple, and **indigo** – the blue form of purple. Often denotes royalty and mysticism.

Step 4

It is important to recognise the significance of the colours on the previous page in a scheme of white, black and neutrals. They can provide the linkage, the separation between colours and are great mixers for all of the above to achieve shades and nuances of colour.

White in all its tints and shades will give you the ability to:
- Make walls recede and therefore make a space look larger.
- Make objects look larger when contrasting with the background.
- Reflect heat.
- Create shadows.
- Provide the separation and emphasis to colours. This is often vital to the success of a scheme.

Black works in direct contrast to white. It will:
- Absorb all light and heat.
- Make walls and objects appear closer than they are.

Black is used to bring visual weight, seriousness and sophistication to a space and is a great contrast to white.

Neutrals: taupes, beige, tones of very pale greys, creams and off-whites. They are:
- Often used to create a quiet effect.
- Used as a background to schemes to provide a harmonious link between strong colours.
- Often used to emphasise form.

Brown comes in many different compositions. It isn't associated with vitality but, if used cleverly, can create a sophisticated edge.

Adding shine to your scheme

My general rule in any scheme, when you feel something isn't working in the space, is to look for its opposite. This could be in the form of colour or visual weight.

Using metals, for example, will often provide that balance and provide attention to detail within the space. It isn't until the lightness and reflective qualities of chrome or stainless steel are added in a kitchen that we feel the effect of it lightening the heavier materials such as wood and stone.

Silver provides your scheme with a reflective, feminine and cool quality. Whether it is in the form of chrome, satin or matt finish, it will bring focus and separation between materials and colours.

Gold provides a masculine statement. It can also create warmth, which silver doesn't. I often use silver and gold together - taking into account proportion and placement.

MATCHING COLOURS TO YOUR MOOD BOARD

As your mood board shows the overall look and style, colour-matching paint samples to your mood board helps you to view the colours alongside the pictures on your board, from the point of view of both hue and tone.

Whether you paint small chips or take them from paint charts (these are available from most home decor and paint stores), colour-match a selection of hues to the mood board. Once you have chosen and cut the paint chips, it is a good idea to place them onto the mood board first to visually match colour and tone. Once you are happy with the match of your colours, place the preferred selection on a separate piece of card in strip format.

Step 4

This palette of colour will be your reference tool for sourcing trips to select hard and soft finishes for the overall scheme.

This is the Jeffries' base palette – a visual reference for the adjectives: natural, textural, casually elegant, nurturing, classic/contemporary, with an element of surprise. Notice how the palette is made up of varying tints and tones to add variety and interest. It is based around an analogous scheme with a complementary accent of red.

DEVELOPING A SCHEME

Let's consider the questions you need to ask when creating your colour scheme.

Room type
- Which aspect or direction does it face?
- How much natural light does the room receive?
- Does the proportion of the room need changing?
- What are your focal points?
- Which elements in the room would you like to minimise visually?
- What atmosphere would you like to achieve?
- What style of living do you wish to convey?
- What is the style of furniture?
- What type of scheme do you wish to employ, i.e. monochromatic, triadic, etc?

MY SEVEN TOP TIPS ON COLOUR

- Match the colour with the mood and function of the room.
- Use warm colours for advancing and cool colours for receding.
- Use the various tints, shades and tones of colour to create variety and character in a room.
- When trying to find harmony in a room, introduce its opposite colour.
- Use the monochromatic, contrasted and related schemes to achieve a harmonious and extended palette.
- Know the colour composition, i.e. what is the undertone of your hue. In this way you can match your finishes.
- Once you have chosen your colour palette consider the proportion and placement in the room.

Once your colour palette has been extracted, half your job is complete. It is now time for you to dress the space, starting with 'Step 5, Selecting your finishes'.

Step 5

SELECTING YOUR FINISHES

Step 5 SELECTING YOUR FINISHES

This is an area where you may be overwhelmed by choice, so it is a good time to be objective when it comes to decision-making on finishes of floors, walls, ceilings etc. You need to ask:

- Will the material be appropriate for the space, its use and atmosphere?
- What impact will it have on the design?
- How much will it cost to buy and install?

A quick decision is not necessarily a good decision. Do your research – it will be worth it. Most finishes will be fixed to the structure of the building. Therefore, once they are laid, they are usually there until the next renovation.

For a perfect and seamless installation, choose the right trades for the job. Specialist materials such as mosaics require specialist fitters – a specialist and expensive material badly installed or laid is a tragedy and can destroy the quality of the scheme! Always ask the supplier of luxury finishes who they recommend to fit these finishes, or to hang them when dealing with luxury wallpapers.

HARD AND SOFT FINISHES

The three most important criteria when choosing finishes is whether they meet your standards in terms of **practicality**, **aesthetics** and **appropriateness**.

As these finishes will be applied mostly to the canvas of the room – wall, floor and ceiling – they will also set the overall tone.

Walls

The walls articulate the space and set boundaries, and are key elements for creating atmosphere, focal points and proportion. If a room doesn't have any discernible features, use the drama of element, theme or focal point to offset the proportion of the room:

- Add detail, such as a dado or picture rail or a bold/patterned wallpaper.
- If the room has too much detail, paint the wall and details the same colour.
- Design the room around a theme or colour scheme.
- Choose a focal point or piece of furniture and apply a bold wall treatment to emphasise. For example, dramatic wallpaper can be used as a backdrop to the focal point of a bed and surrounding furniture.
- Use vertical stripes to change the visual height of a room.

Apart from adding instant character to a room, wall treatments can add practical value. They can insulate from heat and noise, hide imperfections and increase durability. Just remember to specify the right product for the purpose. Corridors and small entrances will need a higher durability than other rooms. To conceal bumps and scratches, a hard wearing scrubbable, vinyl wallpaper is a good solution.

Most wallpapers are **machine printed** and are either spongeable, washable or vinyl. The traditional **hand-blocked** wallpaper is mostly used for historic matching or where specific colourways are required. These are more expensive and will need a minimum meterage, normally 10 m. Further to this, are **silk** wallpapers, which are sometimes finished with embroidery. And as a special art finish, **trompe l'oeil** (deceiving the eye) and **murals** can be commissioned from artists and are also available as wallpaper.

Using fabric on walls is a common feature in Parisian hotels and homes, and is also a successful solution for concealing uneven surfaces, minimising noise reverberation and making a room feel cosy. Because it is applied as a separate surface to the wall, it will physically reduce the dimensions of a room, so make sure you allow for this. Fabric is stretched over batons of wood and insulation fibre.

Floors

The floor not only sets the style and mood of the room, but as it is commonly the largest expanse of material in the room it can also be the most costly. Therefore, the choice should be both a practical and aesthetic one.

Public areas – entrance, living room, kitchen and corridors – will obviously take more footfall than other spaces. Therefore the specification of flooring material should take into account wearability and maintenance/upkeep.

Select your flooring material:
- To suit the tone and mood of your scheme.
- By choosing the colour and texture to harmonise with your scheme.
- By choosing a finish that is easily maintained for the room's use.

Whether wood, stone, ceramic, carpet or leather flooring, consider warmth or coolness, and advancing or receding effects.

Floor material will naturally speak to our senses: the coolness/hardness of stone, the warmth and softness of carpet, the scent of wood and polish, and visual variances of colour, light, texture and pattern. Subconsciously, it can have a cultural resonance, such as terracotta in Tuscan farmhouses, or polished marble in royal palaces. Consider the formality and style of the room when choosing materials.

Design also plays a pivotal role in the dynamics of flooring. When choosing layout, pattern and colourways, use visual viewpoints to create width, narrowness or focus. Texture, light and colour, pattern and line, and the direction and size of tiles or planks, will create visual impact. This can be seen when large tiles are laid diagonally in a galley kitchen, creating energy by their angles and visually enlarging the floor area. Conversely, if tiles are laid parallel to the walls, it will produce a narrowing or more directional effect.

Where there is a transition point – where floors meet, normally at doorways – take into account how materials look together and the height and installation bedding of each product. For instance, a stone floor with bedding will need approximately 20 mm, whereas a flat-weave carpet may only need 15 mm inclusive of underfelt, which is a 5 mm discrepancy. This means the floor base of the carpet will have to be built up. Remember also that you will have to specify the strip of material that covers the seam – this may be metal, wood or rubber. I prefer to match one or other of the materials rather than opting for a metal strip. Don't let the installer decide on this without your approval.

Mixing floor finishes

Another great way of bringing dynamics to the design is by mixing materials, e.g. wood and carpet, leather and metal, leather and wood, etc. The success is in the design, juxtaposition and placement of the materials.

When specifying floor materials between rooms, try to make the transition similar in temperature. Though effective, under-floor heating can be costly – look at more cost-efficient, water-based systems for large spaces and electric matting for smaller spaces.

Method of application

Each material has a method of application that needs a specialist. Always speak with the supplier who will recommend craftsmen they have worked with. Don't skimp on the quality of installation. A poorly installed product will devalue the scheme.

The Jeffries' style is a mix of traditional and contemporary finishes, reflected in the palette.

For the living room, the flooring has been given texture and a period feel with a contemporary form of parquetry, oil-finished to highlight the different wood tones. Added to this, a contemporary selection of rugs define the two seating areas, and bring stability and softness to the zones.

The walls are a combination of period panelling with a leather wall treatment as a backdrop to large pieces of art. The dining area will include a floor-to-ceiling mirror to reflect light and provide impact.

Existing architectural elements of coving and architraves have been painted a warm white, with a hint of green to tone with the walls and flooring.

THE MATERIALS BOARD

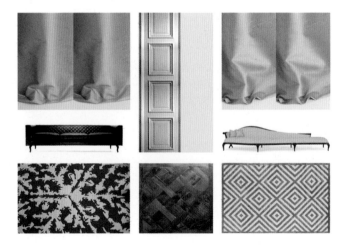

INTERIOR FINISHES SCHEDULE

Area	Element	Description	Finish	Supplier
Living room	Walls	TBA	Leather and wallpanelling	TBA
	Fireplace surround	Full height mirrors	Fixed mirror	TBA
	Ceiling	As existing		
	Floor	Carpet removed		
		Existing parquet re-sanded	Oil finish	TBA
	Architraves	Tatting 1005Y10R	Eggshell	Dulux
	Skirting	Tatting 1005Y10R	Eggshell	Dulux

Take some time to consider your finishes and fill out your own table for your room. You can then follow suit for every other room in the house.

MY SEVEN TOP TIPS FOR SELECTING YOUR FINISHES

- ▶ Choose each finish to enhance the best features of your space and play down the worst.
- ▶ Choose flooring to suit the activity and to set the tone and mood of the scheme.
- ▶ Choose treatments to create character and/or insulate and hide imperfections.
- ▶ Choose finishes with maintenance in mind.
- ▶ Don't skimp on installation costs of finishes.
- ▶ Use colour scheming guidelines for advancing and receding effects.
- ▶ Use pattern and layout to create dynamics and texture.

Now the canvas has been painted/finished, the space is ready to be filled with furniture. This is covered in 'Step 6, Selecting and placing your furniture'.

Step 6 SELECTING AND PLACING YOUR FURNITURE

The classic mistake when selecting furniture is to buy on an emotional whim. It is like shopping for clothes but more expensive. You need to remain focused and review your evaluation, mood board and lifestyle requirements.

You don't want to end up with a sofa that is too large, too soft or hard, or is just not the right colour or texture.

So let's look first at what you have, then decide what you need and would like.

EXISTING FURNITURE

When taking stock of your existing furniture, try to answer the following questions:
- Is the style in keeping with the scheme?
- What is the value of a particular piece to me?
- How comfortable is it?
- Is it worthy of restoration?

If a piece of furniture holds sentimental value and you really love the design, then keep it. Keep the things you love! It may need to be restored or repositioned. Recognise the value of the furniture to you and picture it in the overall scheme. Perhaps it will become a focal point in one of the rooms.

The decision to keep furniture may be made purely on budget, or perhaps on the basis that, with a growing family, it has a shelf life and will do for the time being; you might prefer to invest at a later date.

If it helps, take photographs of the various items and put them on your mood board to help with your decision-making.

OLD FURNITURE

If you want to live in a contemporary environment but have antiques you cherish, mix the furniture but, as with colour, create balance – working on a ratio of 90% contemporary: 10% antique provides interesting focal points. Replacing tired, old upholstery with new colour and texture can enable a piece to fit within a modern setting. Once you add to this a selection of textural or patterned cushions and/or interesting trimmings, it could become the statement piece in the room.

If a chair or sofa needs to be restrung and re-stuffed, always seek out an experienced restorer with empathy for period furniture. You don't want to compromise the design by over-stuffing or making upholstery too rigid/soft. This could destroy the visual line of the furniture.

Before discarding anything in the home, think about changing the use and position of a furniture item instead. When converting an industrial factory to a home, we were left with a pair of old doors. Once they were stripped, sanded and painted, they were successfully re-purposed as dining tables.

NEW FURNITURE

When choosing new items of furniture, have a clear picture in your mind of what you want and what is appropriate and complementary to the scheme. Begin by reviewing the **purpose** and activity of each room, and who will be using it.

So, when buying that new sofa, take into account:
- its level of **comfort** in relation to its required use;
- its **proportion and scale** in relation to room size and height; and
- its **aesthetic appeal** in relation to the scheme and your taste.

Comfort: this is not only about how comfortable the sofa is to sit on but how easy it is to get up from. For example, in a more formal setting, a deep, soft sofa might be too relaxed, but would be perfect in a living room where you wanted to watch films or read.

Scale: this needs to be considered with reference to the proportion of the room. A sofa that seems perfect in an average-sized living room can be completely lost in a large room with high ceilings. An average-sized apartment with low ceilings could not accommodate a large-scale sofa.

However, if space allows, a generous, **low** sofa and chairs around a large coffee table provides a focal point. The emphasis is on luxury of lifestyle rather than apparent lack of space. Always leave room for good circulation and side tables.

Aesthetics: if the design of a sofa doesn't fit into the mood of your scheme, and/or it doesn't personally excite you, don't buy it. Choose one that appeals in line, form, texture and visual weight.

Like mixing colour, mixing styles can add to the vitality and character of the room, so be adventurous. But be mindful of the proportion of each piece sitting next to another – a small, fine bedroom chair without arms would be lost next to a large cushioned sofa.

A statement piece in a carefully chosen complementary colour or texture can be an exciting element of surprise in a room.

PLACEMENT OF FURNITURE

The placement of furniture is just as important as its selection. Grouping furniture in open-plan spaces creates order and intimacy, and defines circulation areas.

Take into account your zoning and activities within the room, reviewing how many you want to seat and the focal points. The layout of furniture should be specific to your needs.

Consider arranging a statement piece of furniture asymmetrically to the seating layout, to emphasise its individuality.

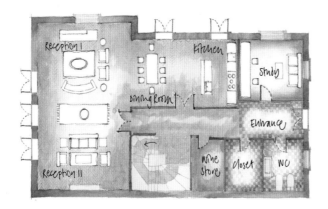

THE JEFFRIES' FURNITURE LAYOUT

The Jeffries thought carefully about where their furniture was placed in order to zone their open spaces, dividing them up for specific purposes.

In their proposed furniture layout above, the two reception areas (receptions 1 and reception 2) are separated by a focal point – a bespoke bronze pedestal table for a marble sculpture sits on a dramatic rug design. Reception 1 offers more individual seating, strategically placed for ease of communication, whereas reception 2 allows for a more relaxed lounging area for viewing television.

The dining area is separated with a generous amount of circulation space between both the reception and kitchen.

The study has been positioned so it is accessible to the entire family.

A wine store and large closet have been included as a late request for more storage and wine tasting room.

The laundry has been relocated to the second floor near to the upper terrace.

The furniture layout in the master bedroom has been arranged to incorporate sleeping, casual seating and a dressing table, in order to create privacy and good circulation. Bedrooms 1 and 2 now have good storage and circulation space, with further space for a desk if required.

The studio and library on the second floor have been divided by a wall of shelving to create privacy, if needed. The guest room is self-contained with a quiet space for reading and access to the kitchen facilities. Placing the laundry on this floor minimises the intrusion of domestic maintenance.

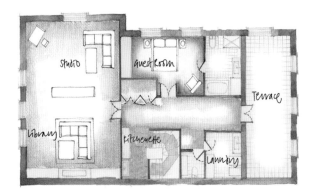

The labels on the floor plan read: Studio, Guest Room, Terrace, Library, Kitchenette, Laundry

Visual zoning can also be achieved by room dividers, either hung from the ceiling or free standing. There are a variety of textural voiles on the market that break up the space transparently without losing sight lines and natural light. Another demarcation technique is to use rugs, relating to the zone and creating focal points.

When placing furniture, consider your viewpoints. If the best outlook from a chair/sofa is of a garden or major piece of artwork, let this be a point of reference when arranging the layout. One often forgets this in a room where an interesting piece of artwork has been used on a particular wall and the other wall has been left bare.

Likewise in the bedroom, which way is the bed facing and what do you look at as you fall asleep and wake up? I could never understand the once-popular mirrored wardrobes placed to one side of the bed. It isn't everyone's desire to see themselves first thing in the morning!

The final test will be obvious when the furniture is in position within the final scheme of the room. Remember that if you compromise on quality or design, it will change the character and atmosphere. Sad but true – 'You get what you pay for'. It may take a few attempts to adjust the furniture in the zones – take time to sit in the chairs, lie on the bed and walk around the furniture to assess viewpoints and comfort of placement.

Step 6

PLANNING THE FURNITURE LAYOUT

For the living room
This is our meeting place in the home. There are a number of activities that can take place here so take into account:

- entertainment – game-related activities on television, games console, cinema;
- how many people need to be seated and therefore the number of chairs or sofas;
- allowance for a reading or quiet area;
- allowance for consumption of drinks and snacks;
- flexibility and quantity of side tables and coffee table; and
- what you will be using the coffee table for and what size is needed.

For the dining room
As the dining room is designed for family and friends to eat together, the layout will need to consider:

- how the food will be served;
- how and when the dining room will be used;
- how many people need to be catered for and seated;
- how much storage is needed for crockery and cutlery;
- tables/consoles for serving; and
- preferences of finish – table and chairs.

For the bedroom
As this is an area of rest, sleep and relaxation, the furniture should support this. The bed, bed-head and surrounds would normally be the focal point and, secondary to these, a dressing table or lounging area. Consider:

- the preferred design and height of the bed, i.e. low-set, high-set, four poster, bed-head;
- preference of material, e.g. wood, metal;
- preference of fabric or material on the bed, e.g. cushions; and
- whether a television is required.

BESPOKE FURNITURE

When standard furniture won't fit into the scheme, either physically or visually, the best option may be to have an item of furniture made to measure (bespoke). In this way you can have exactly what you want in any size, shape, and finish. A bespoke item of furniture will add individuality and uniqueness to your scheme.

Before the bespoke furniture piece is set into production, make sure the manufacturer has clear drawings and samples of fabric. If it is a local factory, visit to discuss the design with the production team, particularly if it is the first time you have used the company.

MIXING UPHOLSTERY

The placement and quantity of colour and texture on the furniture is critical to achieving a cohesive scheme. The juxtaposition of different fabrics on the seats and backs of chairs and sofas can produce some interesting effects.

If you wish to play safe, then stay with the same tone for larger items of furniture and introduce bolder accents on smaller items and cushions. Variations in tone, colour, texture and pattern will produce a layered and more interesting resolution than one colour, tone or texture.

Don't forget the specification for wood tones on furniture legs and side tables, which will need to complement the upholstery and other furniture in the room.

It's a good idea to set up a furniture schedule, nominating each area with type and quantity of furniture. This will highlight what needs to be replaced, what is to be ordered, what has been delivered and what still needs to be sourced.

INSTALLATION

Since many of your items of furniture will be coming from different suppliers, delivery dates will also vary – not everything will arrive on the same day. It is therefore important not to jump to conclusions over the overall cohesion of a space until everything is in place, including secondary items such as lamps, rugs and accessories.

CASE STUDY: THE JEFFRIES' LIVING ROOM FURNITURE

The priority for both reception I and 2 was the seating arrangement needed to be flexible and one or two statement pieces of furniture were to be incorporated into the scheme. Their preference in style was contemporary/classic and favoured finishes of dark walnut wood tones and bronze metals.

A new chaise and chairs were added into reception 1, and a new leather sofa into reception 2. Existing armchairs were restored for use in reception 2. A bespoke bronze pedestal table has been commissioned to feature a newly acquired marble sculpture that sits between the two seating areas. Side and coffee tables were specified in glass and bronze to show off the rug designs to full effect.

FURNITURE SCHEDULE LIVING AREA				
Area	**Element**	**Description**	**Quantity**	**Supplier**
Reception I	Chaise	Mademoiselle – Sophia	1	Christopher Guy
	Sofa	As existing	1	Re-upholstered
	Chairs	TBA	2	
	Coffee table	TBA	1	
	Side tables	TBA	2	
Reception 2	Sofa	Boutique sofa	1	Moooi
	Chairs existing	TBA	2	Re-upholstered
	Coffee table	TBA	1	
	Side tables	TBA	2	

MY SEVEN TOP TIPS FOR SELECTING AND PLACING YOUR FURNITURE

- Review your existing furniture in relation to the requirements of the room.
- Decide to revamp or replace.
- Consider size of furniture in proportion to the room.
- Use the furniture arrangement to create zoned areas.
- Be adventurous – mix styles and/or upholstery.
- When placing furniture, review your viewpoints.
- When buying furniture, consider:
  - comfort
  - proportion and scale in relation to the room
  - aesthetic appeal.

Your furniture is now chosen and the scheme is ready for 'Step 7, Selecting your soft furnishings'.

 **SELECTING YOUR SOFT FURNISHINGS**

It's time for soft texture and character!

Your canvas of materials and finishes on the wall, floor and ceiling are in place, the items of furniture have been chosen and the room is now crying out for softness, texture and the richness of fabrics.

DIFFERENT KINDS OF SOFT FURNISHING

Your soft furnishings include:
- Curtains
- Tie backs
- Blinds
- Bed dressings and throws
- Headboards
- Pelmets/valances
- Cushions
- Wall fabrics
- Upholstered furniture
- Lampshades

Once you are happy with how your scheme is developing, you can continue the evaluation process with fabrics – however, with a little more creativity than objectivity. Soft furnishings provide the softness, texture and richness that make a house a home.

Once you have collated your samples, you may be wondering how you can mix and match the patterns and sizes.

You only have to look at the latest hotels to see that pushing boundaries with the mix of pattern and colours can add freshness and personality to a room. It's really about having the courage to work with it.

What you will notice with many schemes is a sameness in tone of colour and boldness of pattern. For instance, if a large, broad stripe is used on an upholstery, this may be balanced by boldly coloured curtains or furniture size, e.g. lighter or smaller furniture may call for finer silks and patterns.

And there is not only the cover fabric, but also the **lining** (to protect the fabric), **interlining** (to provide insulation), **trimmings** and **accessories** to consider. So don't think that the decision-making is done once you have selected the fabric**.**

You have no doubt seen or experienced the problem: the fabric you viewed in the showroom looks different on the sofa or curtains. It's much the same as the small chip of paint process – the fabric will take on a new life and personality when stretched over sofas and chairs, draped as curtains or hung as blinds.

It also depends on the quantity of the fabric used in relation to other pieces of furniture in the room. Depending on placement it may be bolder or much more subdued. For example, the further away a small printed fabric, the less you will see the pattern and the more subdued will be its colour.

FABRIC SELECTION PROCESS

Before you have anything made up you need to:
- Review and reflect – collate the samples and place them on or next to the mood board you created in Step 1. This helps you see whether your choices match the initial concept.

- Consider your adjectives – does the collection of samples relate to the atmosphere? If you don't want to apply pattern, checks or stripes to larger items of upholstery or curtains, use them as highlights – cushions, throws, or lampshades.
- View the samples *in situ* under varying lights. It is a good idea to ask for returnable samples which are normally a metre long, so you can drape them over the sofa or hold vertically against a window.

For the windows

Choosing fabric to suit the task in the room, the atmosphere and lifestyle, is essential.

Firstly, consider the **use** of the room and design the window treatment to suit. In a kitchen, blinds are normally preferable in case of fire hazard. In bathrooms, steam-resistant fabric, such as laminated roller blinds, normally suit. Bedrooms and living rooms tend to be less restrictive and can be led by design and desired atmosphere.

Take into account what the room will be used for and by whom. If it includes children, you need to know that the fabric withstands stains and isn't easily pulled or snagged. There are some excellent man-made equivalents of more delicate fabrics such as silk that can take wear-and-tear.

The style and atmosphere of each room will influence your choices. Curtains can be the focal point or blended into the colour of the walls. Whether the curtains spill across the floor or 'kiss' the floor (just off the floor) is as much a practical decision as an aesthetic one.

Use colour and pattern to make the statement you want in the room.

A point to remember is that your curtain or blind fabric will be facing away from the window and will therefore appear darker than you perhaps imagined.

For furniture – upholstery

As the furniture provides the form and line, the upholstery provides the texture and colour.

A varied palette used on upholstery and cushions will add character and texture to your room and emphasise focal points, particularly in seating areas. The quality of the upholstery is essential – tight, plump seating, piping that doesn't drift and buttons at even spacing and depth. As an accessory, the cushions should follow suit – there is nothing worse than a cushion that looks half filled or a cushion inner too small for its fabric sleeve.

The effect of a cushioned bed-head and valance at the base of the bed will add the luxury and softness called for in a bedroom. With the addition of textural and patterned cushions, bed coverings and a throw, the nurturing atmosphere is complete.

Cushions should be tactile and detailed to support the scheme. The sizing and quantity is dependent on the size of the bed or sofa. Think of comfort and practicality – you don't want to have to fight to find a space to sit amongst cushions; on a practical note, they also add more back support.

If you wish to enhance the form and line of a piece of upholstered furniture, a plain fabric without pattern may be your best option. This is why a monochromatic choice (as discussed in Step 4) works well with a scheme that is about line and form. Consider the ultra-glamorous Art Deco period scheming, using tones of one colour to show off luxurious textures and form.

To check whether a fabric is suitable for upholstery, take a large sample and give it a good pull in length and width. If it stretches either way, it will stretch and possibly bag when made up as upholstery. You can also check the back of the fabric label where there is normally a diagram of either a curtain or a chair. If it only shows a curtain, then it is not suitable for upholstery. If there is a symbol for both curtains and chair, then it is suitable for both curtains and upholstery.

Step 7

DESIGNING YOUR WINDOW TREATMENT

Choosing your window treatment

Curtains visually soften the edge of the window architrave, obscure or diffuse the light, protect the room from cold draughts and the saturation of light onto furniture, as well as provide privacy.

The practical intention in most rooms, particularly in the northern hemisphere, is to gain natural light without losing heat. With triple glazing and central heating there is no longer the necessity for heavy drapes, unless the design calls for it.

Decide what you need from the window treatment. If you need to shut light out, you may opt for a blackout blind as one layer, and a voile/sheer curtain as a second layer, which will allow diffused light to filter throughout the day, and an insulated curtain in front of the voile for drawing across at night.

Alternatively, a contemporary, casual living room may only require curtains to diffuse the light and provide a textural backdrop. In this instance, the design solution may suit unlined linen curtains, which will also complement a relaxed and contemporary environment.

Next, consider how the window treatment could enhance the **proportion** of the space. Where you place a track or pole can be significant in design terms. If there aren't any proportion issues, then look for height lines of other elements in the room.

However, if you want the windows to look taller or wider, then you can design the window treatment to support this. For example, if height needs to be emphasised in the room, place the track, pole or pelmet closer to the cornice rather than on the window architrave. If this leaves a large blank space above the top of the window, you can either fill this in with a panel of fabric or use this area for stacking the blind. In this way, none of the light is obscured and the overall effect is grander and taller, and creates an interesting overlay of fabrics.

Curtains

You can choose to hang the curtain on a decorative pole or track, or on a combination of both – the decision should be made in line with the overall feel of the room. Would you like to make a feature of it for decorative effect? Then a decorative pole may be the solution. If the room has a more clean-lined, contemporary feel, then a concealed track may be the better solution so not to draw attention to the heading.

The type of heading at the top of the curtain will determine how it falls. Generally, the most common are pinched and cartridged, as the fall from this type of heading works well with most fabrics. If a uniform pleat is required, a version of the 'wave system' (Silent Gliss) works well in contemporary environments. A more casual but effective effect can be achieved with gathering or eyelets, tabs, and loops – they also take less fabric.

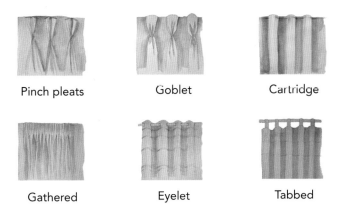

Pinch pleats　　　　Goblet　　　　Cartridge

Gathered　　　　Eyelet　　　　Tabbed

Just remember that heavier fabrics need a decent length of drop for the fabric to fall into folds. For lighter curtains, such as sheer/voiles, weight the bottom corners with coins to avoid them riding upwards at the corners.

Blinds

Where there is not enough room for curtains, or where it is impractical such as in a kitchen, hallway or boat, a blind is a neat option. Choose the type that works with the design and personality of the room. There are various different styles of blinds that roll, concertina or gather up in swathes.

Roller blinds work well as black-out blinds combined with curtains, or can be transparent to replace a sheer/voile curtain. They can also be laminated to avoid the effects of condensation and can be easily wiped down – great for bathrooms.

Roman, cascade, linen fold or London blinds all 'concertina' up or down at varying levels of soft folds. They each also create their own pelmets and can be inset with trimmings to add interest.

London or linen fold

Roller

Cascade

Roman

Shutters

Although strictly not soft furnishings, shutters need to be included as an option for window treatment. Shutters filter light and allow air to circulate through the slats. Aesthetically, the line and shadow filtering through shutters allows for an interesting play of light. Shutters can be painted or varnished to co-ordinate with your scheme. Shutters are also a good option in warmer climates, where use of fabrics may be limited due to high humidity and condensation.

Pelmets and valances

These come in all shapes and sizes and do much to alter the proportion of a window and the character of a room. Functionally, the pelmet is also used to conceal the track and curtain heading.

The pelmet is normally fabric wrapped over board. The valance is without board and therefore less structured. If you are using pelmets, choose a style that works in with your design, paying particular attention to the bottom line, which should reflect the room scheme.

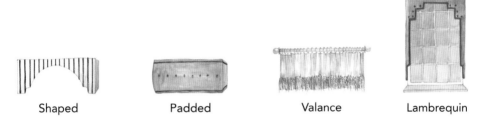

| Shaped | Padded | Valance | Lambrequin |

Another version of the pelmet is the **Lambrequin,** which extends down the sides of the window. It is often used in set design and can be a decorative feature in itself. The Lambrequin is the perfect solution to conceal slithers or cracks of light.

Passementerie and trimmings

Whether used for curtain edges or headings, trimmings (*passementerie* are French-style trimmings) make a statement. For added detail, choose braids, beading, tassels, feathering and leather, relevant to the style of the scheme.

ON SITE

- Check on your survey and notes if there are obstructive details surrounding the window, such as light switches, wall sconces or architectural details, which will need to be taken into account when considering the stacking areas (where the curtains will be drawn back to) of curtains, where blinds can be fitted, where curtain tracks/poles and pelmets can be fitted (wall or ceiling), and where motors can be concealed. Often, in older buildings that have had a commercial use, there may be exposed pipes, electric boxes and other building elements that you need to replace, re-site or remove.

- Meet with all suppliers on site, including curtain makers and upholsterers, if possible. They can then view the extent of the job and advise on issues of making, schedule and installation/delivery. And make sure that if trades people can't visit at the estimation stage they do so before ordering. The order should be subject to suppliers and fitters measuring on site.

- If the product involves automation and technology, it is a good idea to have the builder present at this meeting. For example, electric motors for curtains and blinds will need to be concealed, and there will need to be enough room for tracks and poles.

CASE STUDY: THE JEFFRIES' SOFT FURNISHINGS

The brief for the scheme in the living room was to create casual elegance with an element of surprise. In particular, texture and colour are important to Mrs Jeffries. They have requested tracks and motors for the automation of the curtains be concealed behind a pelmet rather than hiding the headings above a suspended ceiling. The emphasis was to be on individuality – to make the space look like a home not a hotel.

RECEPTION 1 – CURTAINS		
Curtains front on electric track – double fully lined 2.5 times width	Source: Dedar Design: Kipling Width: 138cm	Code/colour: 015 Repeat: N/A
Curtains back on electric track – double unlined 2.5 times width	Source: Sahco Hesslein Design: Griande Width: 138cm	Code/colour: 2445-01 Repeat: N/A

Track	Source: Design: The wave	
Tiebacks	Design: N/A	Code/colour:
Trimming	Velvet	

RECEPTION 1 – UPHOLSTERY

Chaise	Source: Christopher Guy Design: silk supplied	Code/colour: as supplied Repeat: N/A
Sofa	Source: J Robert Scott Design: Bengaline silk Width: 122cm	Code/colour: Blue stack Repeat: 1cm
Cushion	Source: J Robert Scott Design: Edwardian floral Width: 139cm	Code/colour: Indigo Repeat: 72cm horiz 66cm vert
Chairs	Source: Osborne & Little Design: Boxgrove Width: 140cm	Code/colour: NCF4080-01 Repeat: 1cm
Cushion	Source: Lelievre Design: 447-22 Width: 142cm	Code/colour: Cachou – Celadon Repeat: 16cm

RECEPTION 2 – CURTAINS

Curtains front on electric track – double fully lined 2.5 times width.	Source: Dedar Design: Kipling Width: 138cm	Code/colour: 014 Repeat: N/A
Curtains back on electric track – double unlined 2.5 times width	Source: Sahco Hesslein Design: Griande Width: 138cm	Code/colour: 2445-01 Repeat: 26cm

(continued on next page)

(continued from previous page)

Track	Source: Design: The wave	
Tiebacks	Design: N/A	Code/colour:
Trimming	Velvet	
RECEPTION 2 – UPHOLSTERY		
Sofa	Source: Moooi Design: supplied	Code/colour: supplier leather Repeat: N/A
Cushion	Source: Designers Guild Design: Christian Le Quoix Width: 140cm	Code/colour: FCL034/01/C Repeat: 93cm
Chairs restored	Source: Designers Guild Design: Calista Mimosa Width: 138cm	Code/colour: F1985/04/C Repeat: 21cm

MY SEVEN TOP TIPS TO SELECTING YOUR SOFT FURNISHINGS

▶ Consider the palette of soft furnishings as a whole for colour, tone and texture.
▶ Choose fabric for its purpose and practicality.
▶ Use pattern that relates to your theme and adds interest to the scheme.
▶ Decide where to place texture and colour for the benefits of focal points.
▶ For window treatments take into account all of the elements on the window wall.
▶ Decide whether you will conceal or expose curtain headings.
▶ Remember the devil is in the detail when using trimmings.

Having filled your space with furniture and fabrics, it is now time to bring life, vitality and atmosphere into your space with lighting – Step 8.

Step 8 LIGHTING YOUR SPACE

The design and lighting of rooms have been transformed over the last 10 years. Much of this can be attributed to our requirement to use less energy, and to the development of LED (low-energy lighting) and remote technology – controlling the amount and quality of light, and increasing the theatrics and capability of light and source, all at the touch of a button.

Gone are the days of lighting a room with a single pendant or a grid pattern of down-lights with concealed transformers. The technique to create atmosphere remains the same, just with less energy, illuminating for task-related activities and highlighting furniture and objects with a good balance of light and shadow.

Lighting the space has become a science in calculating not only what the light source can do, but how much it will emit and how much energy it will use. It is a good idea to employ the services of a lighting engineer on larger projects as they have the technical expertise, through new, advanced software, in achieving balance, mood and zoning with energy-efficiency formulas.

THE DESIGN

To create light where it is needed, we need to **highlight focal points** and **control the level, quality** and **colour of light.** We want to distribute this as **general**, **task**, **ambient** and **spot** lighting that is suited to the varying times of the day and night.

The height of the room, the focal points and the style and mood you wish to create are key factors to be considered when planning a lighting layout for a room. In this way there can be a play of light and shadow. Work from the perimeter inwards, making sure the edges and walls of the room are illuminated sufficiently, then focus on the elements to be highlighted within the room.

The level of comfort in lighting is achieved by the placement, quality and level of light. Seeing the light source (the light bulb itself) is mostly unnecessary and in most cases produces uncomfortable glare, unless it is a decorative feature in the space.

On stairs the lighting is better placed so the tread itself is washed with light. For safety and comfort, the fittings can be placed at skirting level on the wall. Any additional lighting to the stairwell can be via wall washers and by spot-lighting art and wall features.

Evaluating your room space at the beginning of the project should answer many of the questions a lighting specialist would want to know about your requirements. They also need to know how much natural light will be available in the proposed space and what the aspect is, so that lighting and glare levels can be assessed and the amount of artificial light calculated as necessary.

THE FUNCTION

From a practical viewpoint, the function of lighting a space is based on the **task** and **purpose** of the room. Knowing this will guide you to the right product.

Once the finishes and materials are specified, select your lighting to suit, remembering that dark surfaces will absorb light and light surfaces will reflect. Therefore, the more dark surfaces, the more you will need to increase the level of artificial light.

General lighting
Lighting the circulation areas and zones illuminates the whole room when overall light is called for, and facilitates cleaning.

Task lighting
Task lighting is used where you need light to perform an activity, such as in kitchen areas

used for food preparation, under cabinets and to wash light over the cabinet fronts, as well as inside cabinets to make contents clearly visible.

Ambient lighting

Varying the light levels, using dimmer switches and highlighting specific areas or elements in the room, will create atmosphere. Using light and shadow in the room will highlight and zone specific areas and create mood.

Spot lighting

Should you want to highlight elements such as art, sculpture or interesting furniture or details, these can be emphasised and enhanced with spot lighting.

Quality of specification

Always research your product: new technology attracts new suppliers but not all will be high-quality. This particularly applies to LED lighting. When ordering LEDs, review the quantity, description, colour and the necessary charger or transformer. All these need to be detailed and specified.

LIGHTING DIFFERENT AREAS

Kitchen

Lighting in a kitchen is generally task orientated. However, as the kitchen can also couple up as a casual dining area/bar, ambient lighting could also be added to create atmosphere.

General lighting

Cabinetry will need light to wash the front and inside of cupboards. To illuminate the floor, plinth lighting gently washes light across the floor instead of lighting from above. The **colour** of the light is important, particularly around food. In the kitchen you can see the quality of your raw food, and on the dining table it helps food look appetising.

Task lighting
Lighting workbenches and storage cupboards will create ease and efficiency for the cook. If there are overhead cupboards, design lighting into the base of these to shed light on the backsplash and countertop under the cupboards.

Ambient lighting
Atmosphere can be created by including a decorative pendant and dimmer switches.

Bathroom

The emphasis in a bathroom is on cleanliness and hygiene. Add to this the theatrics of highlighting stone or tiled finishes, as well as low-level soft lighting for ambience. Like the kitchen, the bathroom requires functionality and ambience; as above, you may wish to consider three types of lighting.

General lighting
High-level/overhead general lighting will mostly be switched on for cleaning purposes. Low-level lighting under cabinets washes the floor and countertop with light.

Task lighting
This can be placed around the basin and on shelving and in cabinetry so that contents and depth can be seen easily, as well as in the shower and around the WC and mirror.

Ambient lighting
Plan the placement of light so it doesn't shine down on you when in the bath.

Step 8

Living room

As the living room is for sitting, reading, watching television and entertaining, choose lighting around these activities. If there is a large area or wall of glass, remember that it will appear black at night unless dressed with curtains and/or lighting. If there isn't a curtain, but a view of the garden, use exterior lighting to extend the interior boundaries. Alternatively, if there are curtains, highlight the texture and drape of the fabric with soft lighting.

General lighting
Create light circulation and zoned areas, where necessary, so that an overall level of light is achieved. Avoid any overhead light shining directly into the face or onto the head. Direct lighting onto and around the perimeter of the furniture.

Task and spot lighting
This will highlight artwork, particular pieces of furniture, and/or sculpture, and provide lighting around activities such as reading. Highlight objects and items of interest on tables or mantlepiece and any artwork on the walls.

Ambient lighting
Freestanding up-lights or table lamps not only add atmosphere but create good diversity of height, form and texture.

Bedroom

The placement and spillage of light should be designed so that it minimises sleep disturbance, provides soft lighting for winding down and task lighting for reading. Lighting on dimmers, either remote or switch, should be easily accessed from bed and on entering the room.

General lighting
This will provide an overall light for circulation and cleaning purposes.

Task and spot lighting
This will be needed around areas for reading, dressing and perhaps watching television, especially if there are any objects or artwork, interesting textural fabric or wallpaper you want to highlight.

Ambient lighting
This will create mood. Consider the various focal points in the room, such as the bed-head and surrounds, and lounging area, to set the mood lighting.

Entrance

The purpose of the entrance is to meet and greet, take coats and luggage. It may also have a cupboard to house electrics and technology systems.

General lighting
Use a few down-lighters to provide overall illumination. This will enable you to see the whole space on entering for practical and security purposes. From an aesthetic viewpoint, the entrance is the space to make an all-important design statement.

Task and spot lighting
This category also becomes functional, as the entrance door will need to be sufficiently illuminated both on the outside and inside. Look for your best features and highlight them.

Ambient lighting

The atmosphere of the entrance should provide a visual interpretation of the rest of the house. If the space is narrow and without much natural light, it is a good idea to include focal points, such as art or a large mirror, to create definition and a sense of spaciousness.

Corridors

Hallways and corridors can often look monotonous and soulless, or have too many doors interrupting the space. Look for the best features, or add an interesting design on the floor or walls and highlight as focal points.

General lighting

Washing the walls with light will expand the space visually and illuminate the parameters.

Task lighting

Spot lighting art or a floor design will add interest and focal points within a hallway. If there is an interesting cornice or ceiling feature, highlight this to visually heighten the space.

Ambient lighting

The combination of interesting focal points, decorative pendants or sconces and low and high level lighting will bring interest and proportion to the corridor.

External space

Taking in the boundaries of the garden is an excellent means of visually expanding your internal living space. Remember to take into consideration the internal living decoration when planning garden lighting.

General lighting
The garden is the area to combine circulation with security lighting, i.e. along paths and in dark spots. This can be a light-sensitive control system, whereby lighting automatically switches on when you enter.

Spot lighting
Create focal points by lighting trees, shrubbery, sculpture or a pond, hiding the light source inside foliage.

Ambient lighting
Depending on the theme of the garden, and as with the internal decoration, you may wish to introduce decorative lamp lighting.

The Jeffries chose a mixture of subtle and decorative lighting for the main living areas. Wall washers will show up the texture of curtains and spotlight the artwork providing a perimeter to the room. Seating areas will be lit by central pendants over coffee tables supplemented by floor lamps. The dining room will have a statement chandelier pendant.

The example schedule below lists the lighting and its quantity.

LIGHTING SCHEDULE					
Area	**Element**	**Description**	**Finish**	**Quantity**	**Supplier**
Living room/ Reception 1	New pendant	Repair existing rose	Bronze and amber glass	1	TBA
	Down lights	Existing removed & replaced with LED wall washers		8	TBA
	Table lamps formal	Hand-blown textured glass with horsehair shades/gold interior		2	TBA
	Table lamps living	Hand-blown coloured glass with horsehair shades/silver interior		2	TBA

MY TOP SEVEN TIPS FOR LIGHTING YOUR SPACE

▶ Light with the planet in mind – where you can, use LED.
▶ Create mood and atmosphere with a considered lighting plan.
▶ Light for task and focal points – choose activities and lighting to accentuate furniture or art.
▶ Light for ambience – use theatrics to add variety and accents.
▶ Light for decoration – create a design statement to enhance the theme, such as a chandelier, pendant or table lamps.
▶ Light for general purposes, such as circulation.
▶ Consider purpose of space and light to suit.

Now that you have dealt with the theatrics of lighting, it is time to accessorise and to fill your space with your signature pieces. The placement and display of these items will be as important as lighting them. We look at this in 'Step 9, Styling and accessorising your space'.

 STYLING AND ACCESSORISING YOUR SPACE

Styling is the opportunity to show your taste and style, your unique collection of art, objects and family history. But it is the placement of the collection that will make the difference!

Just as adding cushions to a sofa softens the block colour, so, too, the elements of art, vases, sculpture and glass, metal and texture, depict the character. Before accessories are added to a room, it can all too easily look like a furniture showroom. Your style of accessories will liven up dark or uninteresting areas in a space and balance out the visual weight of a room.

Your prize possessions – what do they say about you?
As you unpack some of your prize possessions and collectables, it's time to ask the question – what does it say about you? This is also the time for you to **review** and **revise** and perhaps **let go**.

If you don't have much of a collection, it's time to go shopping! Before setting out, think about every room.

As you unpack some of your prize objects and collectables, a piece of your soul is being revived and can now be expressed.

Display art and photos to match the mood of your room
- The placement of art or objects allows you to review each space with a fresh and objective eye. Don't be caught up in placing on the basis of familiarity. Assess the mood in each room and match it with the piece of art or an object to suit.
- Displaying art and photos should be dependent not only on the mood of the room but also on how you want it to be perceived and by whom. For instance, if your home is a mix of business and personal guests, you may wish to house a family photo collection in a less public space, such as on a stair landing. In this way it will be the guests/friends entering these spaces who will appreciate the family history.

- The presentation of a collection of photos in frames isn't about the size of the frame but the general cohesion. Choose a frame to enhance the subject and not vice versa. The frame shouldn't overpower the picture or interior scheme.
- When displaying art, remember to hang it at a height that is not a strain to view. Hanging artwork and pictures is dictated by the measurement on the wall from the floor in relation to furniture arrangements. Align the centre of the picture to the eye level of the viewer. If it is a double hang, the aim is to have the centre point between the two pictures. However, if the picture is hung over a low sofa or table, you may need to hang the picture lower than normal to keep a relationship between the picture and furniture setting.
- Always assess whether it's the furniture or the art that needs to be moved before puncturing the wall with hooks. Alternatively, if you don't wish to puncture the wall, or you have an evolving collection of art, hang from a picture rail. It is also possible to conceal the picture rail into the cornice.

The element of surprise

Pushing the boundaries breathes a sense of excitement into rooms.

- Look to add a surprising detail to revive blandness and add a sense of drama.
- The eye is drawn to good and bad detail, which can make or break a scheme – the devil is in the detail!

ACCESSORISING ROOMS

Entrance

Once the practicalities of storing coats and/or luggage have been taken care of, your visitor inevitably receives a visual and first impression of your home via the entrance and the viewpoints beyond.

- A statement piece, whether a vase of flowers, large mirror or piece of art or sculpture, will provide a focal point in large and small spaces.
- Mirrors act as good light reflectors in dark corridors, but always take into account what the mirror will be reflecting.

Kitchen

As this is generally the centre hub of the house, it needs to support your lifestyle and harmonise with the rest of the scheme, particularly in open-plan settings.

- It needs to be both practical and comfortable for preparation and cooking and perhaps casual dining.
- Offset the visual weight of materials such as stone and wood with hardware or accessories that bring reflection and light into the scheme.
- When the kitchen is an extension of the living room, accessorise to complement and unify both spaces.
- A piece of art, glassware or ceramics will add interesting focal points and character to a room.

Dining room

Dining with friends and/or clients is an experience for them to share a part of your lifestyle. You can therefore create an atmosphere and mood to represent you – the style of food, the way it is served, together with furniture, the style of tableware, centre table piece, the art or mirror on the wall, placemats, serving dishes, cutlery.

- Take into account viewpoints from every seat around the table, and place art, mirrors and the orientation of the dining table to create interest.
- Remember your best dining experience and emulate the setting.

Living room

Whether formal or casual, the living room is intended for relaxed entertainment, social interaction and comfort. Remember that:

- Once you have established your focal points, add accessories to emphasise.
- The fireplace is the obvious starting point where objects can be arranged on the mantlepiece. Try for a less contrived look by placing items asymmetrically.
- You need to consider the elements on the coffee table – a pair of small candles combined with a selection of artefacts or interesting coffee table books and magazines. Choose accessories that will bring life and interest to the elements around it.

Bedroom

Depending on the size of the bedroom, there will be zoned areas and a number of activities. Normally, the bed is the focal point and the perfect opportunity to make a statement, from luxurious opulence to textured simplicity. A secondary focal point may be a lounging area with reading light and coffee table.

- A layering effect of texture and colour will add visual comfort to the room.
- The style of cushions and throw will add to the comfort and tone.
- Think about placement and storage of personal accessories, such as mobile phones and chargers.
- Practical objects, such as a water bottle and glass, can be design pieces; the placement needs to be both practical and aesthetic.
- Consider whether you would like any additional items, such as free-standing suit hangers or wall hooks.

Bathroom

The bathroom or en suite has evolved from a purely utilitarian washing room to a space of indulgent pampering. It has also become the ultimate fashion statement.

- Choose accessories that reflect the tone and quality of the bedroom.
- Consider the accessories: shaving mirrors, bins, towel storage and soap dispensers.
- The selection and style of accessories can add the sparkle of glass, mirror or metal or the textural softness of towels or other objects.

TIME FOR YOUR OVERVIEW

To overview your collection of accessories, inclusive of art and photos, do a 'walk through' of each room and take photos for reference. Any areas that need further work and more accessories need to be noted. These notes and pictures can then be referred to on sourcing trips.

After placing all of your accessories, review your room with a critical eye, taking into account the balance of the display in terms of form, height and collective structure. If you find problems with balance, try to counterbalance with its opposite.

- If there are sections of the room that are either too dark or too light, look for its complement as a contrast.
- Lighten up a heavy scheme with glass, chrome or textural ceramics.
- Look at the varying heights within the room to add more vitality and interest.

The atmosphere and finish should be in line with your initial vision when you created the mood board in Step 1. Have you achieved your dream interior?

Of course, one could say that once the accessories and styling is over the job is complete, but I would like you to consider that this journey is ever evolving.

Due to being avid art and object collectors, the problem was not about what to place but where. Some pieces of art were given new homes in different rooms, and the emphasis on creating focal points with sculptural objects quickly brought textural variety and a range of heights into the room.

A photo gallery was created in the hallway, while a few interesting pieces of glassware added to the sparkle of the room. One marble sculpture was introduced into receptions 1 and 2 on a bespoke bronze hall table, and the house finally became a home. The newly designed section of the house has been minimally accessorised, allowing the Jeffries, as avid collectors, to add to the arrangement. In this way, the personality of the rooms will evolve as they collect on their travels.

The element of surprise varied in each room, from smaller details of contrasting buttons, trimmings and oversized headboards in the bedrooms, to bespoke, artisan pieces of furniture, finishes on walls and bespoke textiles, to complement or replicate the artwork.

MY SEVEN TIPS FOR ACCESSORISING YOUR SPACE

> Display collectables as a grouping to emphasise the subject.
> Make a statement about your taste.
> Identify the element of surprise.
> Enhance your focal points.
> Complement the mood in each room with the style and placement of accessories.
> Assess the balance and structure of your accessories to create variety.
> The devil is in the detail – make it right.

Now let's put everything into action on site with 'Step 10, Planning your work programme', and creating the team you wish to work with.

Step 10

PLANNING YOUR
WORK PROGRAMME

Step 10 PLANNING YOUR WORK PROGRAMME

Despite our best intentions, we all have a tendency to look at the cost of a project and then how we can cut corners to bring it down. And project management seems to be one of the first areas that home owners think they can manage. Most often, the end result of running a project yourself is more expense. You may end up spending more time and money patching up the mistakes, retracting on bad decisions and/or underestimating time and labour. Where you intended to save, you have had to spend to make good. A project manager will take the responsibility and burden of all works and deliveries on site.

The complexity and need for consistency of decision-making and communication with trades and professionals on a project is vastly underestimated.

'Design without planning your work programme at your own peril.'

It can take you by surprise just how long a project can take. Waiting for planning approval from your local council can take months. Importing products and having items tailor-made as bespoke pieces also takes time. Remember to always build in reality checks on the project, labour and products.

My rule of thumb is: estimate a project cost and timescale and double it – this takes into account unknown variables and the labour content attached to them. In this way, you will be pleasantly surprised if the overall job is under budget and within time.

OUTLINING THE SCOPE OF WORKS

Before taking steps to design your space, you will need to consider just what is involved. This will enable you to communicate your brief to professions and trades and list the parameters of the project.

The project

The project on site needs structure, a programme and a great team (professional and trades) working with you to achieve the best and final result. A list of what needs to be done will outline the scope of the works. Drawings showing existing and proposed works, and schedules listing the products being installed, are essential.

The process

Depending on the complexity of the project, the design development stage can vary. Delays happen for varying reasons but the most time-consuming is waiting for planning approval, and/or evaluation of the structural support. Meetings on and off-site need to be scheduled as quickly as possible to obtain approval, after which the building works can progress again. Typically, the building/refurbishment process for a house can take one year to 18 months, or, for an average-size apartment, three to six months.

Also, be aware of local council regulations in your area – be prepared for the cost of a skip, its license and the need to apply for a parking bay suspension. The longer you require the skip the more expensive it becomes per day.

The following table is an example of the areas to consider as you prepare.

The Brief or Proposal	Describing what you intend to do Planning approval – requires drawings
Demolition	To enable works to be secure and not disruptive to the street, hoardings may need to be erected.
Construction	This includes walls, doors, any new building works If roof work is required, scaffolding can be erected once the structure is complete.

(continued on next page)

(continued from previous page)

Services	Plumbers and electricians will need to disconnect existing services if work is needed for:
	    plumbing
	    gas/hot & cold water supply
	    heating and ventilation
	    electrical supply & lighting
	    telephones & media
	    security systems

Floors	New areas of slab, screed and any new finishes
Ceilings	New ceilings and cornices
Windows	Schedule of windows
Doors/ironmongery	Schedule of doors
Lighting	Types of fittings and positioning
Bathrooms Kitchens	Types of fittings and positioning
Fitted furniture	Positioning of each item of furniture
Finishes/decoration	A schedule nominating each finish, preparation required and where it will be positioned
Window treatments	A schedule listing the window treatment for each window, the supplier and date required on site
Loose furniture	A furniture schedule listing all loose furniture, supplier and position on plan
Accessories	A schedule listing all artwork, mirrors and objects and position in each room

The quotation/estimate process

In much the same way as you have created a brief for your vision, you will need to brief your supplier and contractor on your requirements and objectives. The supplier, craftsmen and contractor need to have a clear idea of what you want to achieve.

You will need to provide:
- dimensions to enable suppliers to provide an estimate/quotation;
- a deadline for the project so they can establish whether their production team can commit to this; and
- site details to trades so they can provide delivery costs.

The ordering process

Once you have received the quotation, you can turn this into an order. Whether you take the responsibility of placing the order yourself or leave it to the building team is your choice. If you place the order, the responsibility for the supervision of process and delivery is yours.

First fix (installation)

The first fix includes the installation of walls, plumbing and electrical work, and window and door spaces, which are built in before the dry lining (insulation and plaster boarding) is fixed. The walls can then be plastered and skimmed, bathrooms are tanked and tiled, and skirtings, architraves, internal doors, built-in wardrobes and shelves can be built in.

Second fix (installation)

This stage includes installing all fixtures in bathrooms and kitchens and the electrics and plumbing to support this. It is also at this stage that radiators are plumbed in.

After this the decorative finishes can be applied to all rooms.

ON-SITE DELIVERY CHECK LIST

Having received the delivery of items, particularly if there are a number of multiple items such as taps, compare the order with the stock that has arrived to check quantity, colour and quality.

Kitchen/bathrooms
Do a thorough check to see that everything is working well and there aren't any chips in stone surfaces or cupboard fronts. Check that drawers slide freely and that the finishing inside and out is as you would expect.

Lighting fixtures
Check that the placement of switches has been done accurately, at the right height and level.

Furniture
Check that all woodwork is clear of dents or scratches, all metal finishes have no scratches and the upholstery is fitted correctly, is unmarked and the correct fabric.

Soft furnishings
Check that cushions and trimmings are as you expected, for example that the cushions are plump and well made, and that piping, trimmings and buttons are correctly positioned.

Check that curtains have been set at the right height, the drop is as you had specified, whether 'kissing' or spilling onto the floor, and that hemlines are straight. Check that stitching is invisible where necessary and that you are happy with the pleating.

Check all accessories, ombres or tie backs have been set at the correct height.

Snagging
This is the final walk around with architect and site manager to checklist all defects.

MY SEVEN TOP TIPS WHEN PLANNING YOUR WORK PROGRAMME

- Provide a thorough outline of your brief and stick to it.
- Make sure the team of tradesmen and professionals are available to work on the project from start to completion.
- Keep good communication and provide regular updates to everyone on site.
- Ask trades to keep the site clean.
- Provide secure storage for items delivered prior to installation.
- Make sure every item to be delivered can fit through doorways.
- Do a thorough snagging list on completion.

 THE COMPLETED PROJECT

At this final stage, I hope you still feel the excitement and desire to transform your environment to suit your needs. Remember, it's about knowing your strengths and weaknesses and what you are prepared to take on. The decision to go it alone or bring in the professionals will be up to you.

My intention in writing this book has been to give you a general framework via a 10-step process to help you with your project. I hope this helps you to see which areas you would enjoy managing yourself and which areas you might want to call in the services of a professional.

I'm sure you would want to know the outcome of the Jeffries' project.

THE FINAL OUTCOME FOR THE JEFFRIES' PROJECT

You may remember that the Jeffries' initial request was for design supervision only. Like many, they thought they would be hands-on with project management. But as the project progressed, it became evident that they had 'bitten off more than they could chew' and did not have the time or experience to manage the project themselves. They very wisely decided to appoint a building contractor with project manager.

This made all the difference. They followed my advice and met with a team of professionals and relevant trades once a week to inspect and discuss any issues on site, drawing up requirements and/or any changes to the programme. The professional management and supervision of the project helped keep the completion date on track and everything else, from design supervision to quality assessment, in check.

I was there with the expertise and experience to suggest the best solution to planning, specification and selection of items that went into each space. As I had led them to expect, planning approval to replace windows to French doors took six weeks, inclusive of site visit by the council.

Employing a project manager proved to be a great investment. Unfortunately, a few pieces of furniture from Italy were delayed because of vacation clashes. However, as they had been ordered well in advance the delay did not affect the completion date (it is all down to good organisation).

The whole job, which we anticipated would take nine months, extended to 10 months.

How did the Jeffries feel?

The collaboration between the Jeffries and myself was based on mutual trust, respect and open communication.

The Jeffries feel they got the best of both worlds. They felt their input was valued and appreciated, and the experience of having a professional designer on board meant they avoided many expensive pitfalls.

They feel that their home is now unique and reflects their lifestyle.

Were there any lessons learned along the way?

Like most people, the Jeffries could visualise their lifestyle but did not know how to achieve it. Once this had been resolved in the planning stages, their confidence and enthusiasm grew.

Every project presents new challenges and a different resolution. But remember that if the solution is greater than your experience, bring in the professionals. Most of us take on a project with enthusiasm and then start to flounder, because life and inexperience gets in the way.

The final resolution

Never underestimate the value of experienced professionals and the expertise they can bring to your project. Check each decision on-site is in line with your design brief.

How successful was the project?

The Jeffries have embraced their new space and now have a home they love and a scheme that expresses their taste. It's a space that, as a family, they can grow and evolve in.

And, as for the future, I'm about to design their villa in Tuscany!

A final word   IT'S YOUR JOURNEY

Having led you through the journey of transforming your interior, it is now time to make the decision whether to **'go it alone'** and risk making all the common mistakes mentioned in this book, or **work with a professional** to ensure that you get exactly the dream space you are seeking without the stress lying heavily on one pair of shoulders. Ultimately, you have made the decision to embrace change and take control of your environment, to express yourself and to create a home that supports your needs.

I love transforming people's lives by creating interiors that fit their needs, their lifestyles and their aspirations. And everyone is different! I want you to live in the space you deserve, build your sanctuary and present your statement to the world. In this way, you are not only transforming your house, you are transforming your life!

As a reminder and checklist, I have summarised the steps covered in this book:

STEP 1: EVALUATING YOU

Evaluate where you are *now* and where you *want* to be. If your home isn't expressing who you really are, then take the opportunity and change it. Remember that where and how you live is your statement to the world of how you feel about yourself, so why not express the real you?

Transforming your environment is investing in yourself and will affect the quality of your life, your psychological wellbeing and increase the value of your property. List your preferences for the lifestyle you want and create a visual image of your dream lifestyle.

STEP 2: EVALUATING YOUR SPACE

An evaluation of what exists requires a survey of the following:

- current use of the space
- best and worst features of the space
- requirements for change
- dimensions of the room – width and length
- ceiling height
- door and window dimensions
- elevations of walls, noting power sockets and architectural elements.

Most homes and spaces can be divided into public and private areas, whereby public areas are used more frequently and by more people and private areas are designed to be more intimate and quiet.

Finally, make a list of what you would like from each space and the key items you require.

STEP 3: DESIGNING YOUR SPACE

Remember that the new design and layout is for the comfort and convenience of everyone using the rooms. Make the best of existing features and elements. Decide what can be removed or re-sited and/or how spaces can be enlarged or re-shaped to accommodate your needs.

Appendix

The financial outlay and the time and upheaval to change your space should remind you that this is not something you will want to change for some years to come, so evaluation of your needs and requirements prior to this phase is crucial.

When planning your layout, take into account:

- requirements for future growth so that your family can expand and grow into the space
- needs of technology and storage in every space
- viewpoints internally and externally
- focal points in each room.

STEP 4: CHOOSING YOUR COLOUR PALETTE

Understanding and making decisions on colour is an emotional one. When you use tried and tested colour combinations and realise the emotional impact that this can create, you can devise a scheme that creates the desired atmosphere.

Take note of colour attributes: lightness, darkness, brightness. When a room feels overloaded with one of these attributes, try using a contrast or opposite to create balance.

When matching colours, look for the hues composed in one colour. For example, if a stone has a green-grey base, whites used with this should contain a hint of green rather than blue or yellow.

If the proportion of a room is problematic, use colour, pattern and texture to change it visually. For example, to make a room look wider or higher, use different shades, tints and saturation of colour along with pattern and design.

Always consider the placement and quantity of colour. Once you know your focal point in the room you can draw the eye to that point by using colour, remembering that warm colours advance and cool colours recede.

STEP 5: SELECTING YOUR FINISHES

When choosing finishes always consider the tone and character of the room style over what is in trend. Then review the purpose and function of the room and choose the product accordingly.

Before specifying a product, consider its:

- practicality
- aesthetic appeal
- appropriateness.

Remember to consider your transition points when selecting finishes, for example where flooring meets doorways. Take into account the height difference of products and/or underlay thickness, and consider the juxtaposition of pattern and colour.

Try not to be caught up in the latest trends. Rather, look for the product that will enhance the scheme and be the best solution for the purpose of the room.

STEP 6: SELECTING AND PLACING YOUR FURNITURE

Whether your furniture is old or new, the most important considerations should be:

- comfort
- proportion and scale
- style and aesthetic appeal.

The selection of furniture should be:

- suited to the purpose
- appropriate to the scheme.

Placement of furniture should take into account:

- the activity within the room or space
- how many people will need to be catered for
- viewpoints
- don't be afraid to mix styles.

Remember 'you get what you pay for'.

STEP 7: SELECTING YOUR SOFT FURNISHINGS

The function of the soft furnishings palette is to reveal form, provide tactile comfort physically and visually, and to provide emphasis and cohesion through the selection and placement of colour. And don't forget the practicality of the chosen fabric – you don't need silk around children, there are plenty of good imitations.

Review the function of the room, your focal points and use the soft furnishings to emphasise and enhance. Use accents to emphasise detail and add interest to your scheme. For example, a window's proportion can be changed or corrected with the use of clever window treatment. This will also add character and cohesion to the other textural elements in the room.

Remember that 'the devil is in the detail', so make sure that your cushions, throws, upholstery, and trimmings are designed and made to perfection.

STEP 8: LIGHTING YOUR SPACE

The level of comfort in lighting your space is achieved by:
- placement
- quality of light source
- control of light emitted.

Light your space to:
- create mood and atmosphere
- emphasise focal points
- take into account task-orientated activities
- add variety and theatrics to your space
- introduce decorative and design lighting
- control the colour and quality of light
- provide general lighting for circulation.

Review the function of the space and base your lighting plan around the task or purpose of lighting in that area.

STEP 9: STYLING AND ACCESSORISING YOUR SPACE

Adding the accessories of art, photographs, and objects is an expression of you. It is your final signature and statement about who you are, what you like to collect and where you have travelled.

When placing accessories, consider:
- the mood and atmosphere you wish to create in the room
- your focal points
- the display of the collection.

And remember that all-essential **element of surprise!**

STEP 10: PLANNING YOUR WORK PROGRAMME

Your work programme requires:
- the team to build and install the project
- a work programme and paperwork to carry out the work
- a realistic timeline.

The team:
- decide on your professional team
- create a team of trades people
- decide who will project manage the job.

The project:
- draw up a brief
- list the areas and work needing to be done
- review what drawings and schedules will be required.

On-site:
Remember to check every delivery for quantity, colour and quality as it arrives on-site.

Credits and Acknowledgements

CREDITS

Front cover and mood board, page 29:

Sculpture by Emily Young, courtesy of The Fine Art Society, London. Photography Angelo Plantamura, w: www.shootingart.co.uk

Wallpaper: Fornasetti II Procuratie by Cole & Son. Photography Joakim Blockstrom, w: www.cole-and-son.com

Image of icicles, 123RF Stock Photo: w: http://www.123rf.com/photo_7551693_icicles-on-tree-branch.html

Other Stockists – Furniture, Lighting, Finishes, Textiles, Accessories

Textiles

DEDAR (UK) LTD, Unit C7 – Design Centre East Chelsea Harbour Design Centre London SW10 0XF, t: +44 (0)20 7351 9939, w: www.dedar.com; http://homefabricshermes.dedar.com.en

DESIGNERS GUILD, w: www.designersguild.com

OSBORNE & LITTLE, 304 King's Road London SW3 5UH United Kingdom, w: www.osborneandlittle.com

SAHCO HESSLEIN UK LTD, G24 Design Centre Chelsea Harbour GB – SW10 0XE London, t: +44 (0)20 7352 6168, e: info@sahco.co.uk

J ROBERT SCOTT, Unit 114, First Floor, North Dome, Chelsea Harbour Design Centre, Chelsea Harbour Dr, London SW10 0XE, t: (0)20 7376 4705, www.jrobertscott.com

LELIEVRE UK, Chelsea Harbour Design Center, London SW10 OXE, t: +44 (0)20 7352 4798, e: enquiries@lelievre.eu

Furniture

MOOOI, www.moooi.com

ALISON CLAIRE, alison claire ltd. The White Building, 555 Harrow Road, London W10 4RH, t: (0)20 8962 5691, e: ivana@alisonclaire.com, w: www.alisonclaire.com

CHRISTOPHER GUY, Hampton Business Park, Unit 4, Hampton Road West, Middlesex TW13 6DB, t: +44 (0)20 3397 2410, e: uk@christopherguy.com, w: www.christopherguy.com

Flooring
COLBOURNS – Hand Tufted Carpets & Rugs, Studio 11, 65-69 Lots Road, SW10 0RN, t: +44 (0)20 7352 8335, w: www.colbourns.com

THE RUG COMPANY, 124 Holland Park Avenue, London W11 4UE, t: (0)20 7229 5148, w: www.therugcompany.com

NAJAUTZON POPOV TEXTILES, designed by Naja Utzon Popov, w: www.najautzonpopov.com

Finishes
ROCKET ST GEORGE, t: +44 (0)1444 253391, w: www.rockettstgeorge.co.uk

Lighting and Accessories
VESSEL, Vessel Gallery, 114 Kensington Park Road, London W11 2PW
UK, t: +44 (0)20 7727 8001, w: www.vesselgallery.com
Balustrade Centre piece by Simon Moore for Vessel Editions

India Stacking Vessels by Pia Wüstenberg

KATHY DALWOOD, t: 020 7372 2677, e: kathy@kathydalwood.com,
w: www.kathydalwood.com; www.kathydalwood.blogspot.com
Plaster busts:
Mme Sacre Coeur, height 36cms
Tower Bridge Dragoon
36cm

Credits and Acknowledgements

ACKNOWLEDGEMENTS

Sheelagh McNamara – for her enthusiastic support and professional feedback.

Lisa Ferguson, Di Collins, Ingrid Silver, Carole Maxwell for reviewing.

Judy Dendy – for her help in editing my book.

Sue Richardson Associates (SRA Books) – for perfecting the end result.

Lucy Daniels – Dippy Egg Illustrations – book illustrations.

The KPI team, Kelly Clifton and Gina Hardy – who inspired me to write the book.